Saving the Pitcher

SAVING THE PITCHER

Preventing Pitching Injuries
in Modern Baseball

WILL CARROLL

Ivan R. Dee
CHICAGO

Graphs created by baseballgraphs.com. Anatomical drawings from Joseph Sheppard, *Anatomy: A Complete Guide for Artists*, courtesy of Dover Publications.

www.ivanrdee.com

The paperback edition of this book carries the ISBN 1-56663-728-7.

Library of Congress Cataloging-in-Publication Data:
Carroll, Will, 1970–
  Saving the pitcher / Will Carroll.
    p. cm.
  ISBN 1-56663-578-0
  1. Baseball injuries. 2. Pitching (Baseball) 3. Sports injuries. 4. Sports medicine. I. Title.
  RC1220.B3C376 2004
  617.1'027—dc22

2004043848

To the women: Barbara, Lois, Anne, Virginia,

and the angel on my shoulder, Jessica

Contents

Preface

If pitching is half of baseball, analyzing pitching is half controversy. Since beginning my work in the field of injury analysis, I've seen my share of controversy, acrimony, and disdain. While attempting to do two things—bring new light to the field of sports medicine in baseball, and analyze injuries in the way that sabermetrics analyzes on-field performance—I've been labeled controversial. I've called people out about lying in the media. I've written the truth about situations when everyone else was printing the party line. Despite my work on injuries, I'm probably best known for an article I wrote (with Derek Zumsteg) regarding Pete Rose's attempted return to baseball. But I'm tired of that story.

In this book I stick to the facts and try to do what I set out to do in the first place: analyze the available data and attempt to make baseball a better game.

As you'll see in the book, the game is hurt by injuries, both on the field and in the wallet. Not only are major league teams losing days and dollars to injury, some players who might be the next Clemens, Johnson, or Prior are on a high school or college field somewhere . . . and their elbow is sore. They've been overworked, undertrained, and are tired. They want to be the best and they may have the talent, but forces conspire against them. No one is protecting their arm, not through any dark desire to see them fail but because of the wrongheaded "wisdom" of past generations, passed down to do damage like some cursed heirloom.

In collecting the knowledge, research, and common sense you'll find here, I've also managed to write some things sure to promote an argument. Here, for example, are some of the ideas you'll find in this book.

- I don't believe in curveballs or sliders.
- The most important part of a pitcher isn't his arm.
- There's no reason a pitcher should ever be injured.
- Most pitching coaches don't have a clue about pitching.
- Pitch counts are overrated and tell us almost nothing.
- More pitchers are ruined in high school than anywhere else.
- Steroids are as much a problem in pitching as they are in any other sport.
- Players can be taught to be pitchers.

Dr. Mike Marshall, one of the great pitching coaches in this or any era, and a Cy Young Award winner himself, said to me in an interview that if pitchers would just do things the way he teaches them, he could eliminate pitcher injuries. He's right.

You can find other books on all the subjects I write about here. Videotapes, camps, and websites teach some of the things I'll write about. What makes this book different is that in the course of writing my column for Baseball Prospectus and working with the amazing group of analysts there, I've been able to learn who is worth listening to. I've learned who gets results and who is doing the groundbreaking work that will change the game.

This book brings it all together, in hopes that the entire body of knowledge laid out for you will help save one pitcher—perhaps you, perhaps your son, or perhaps the ace of your staff.

Please note that throughout this book I use the masculine pronoun. I do it chiefly for reasons of economy. The same basic scientific principles apply to women. For overhead throwers in any sport, there is very little difference in mechanics between males and females.

Saving the Pitcher

1

SAVING THE PITCHER

On a warm August afternoon in 1998, a young pitcher named Kerry Wood exploded into the national consciousness and the hearts of Cub fans everywhere by tying the major league record for most strikeouts in a game. Just two years out of a high school in suburban Texas, Wood became the latest in a long line of Texan flamethrowers. His twenty strikeouts pushed his name onto the list with his boyhood heroes, Nolan Ryan and Roger Clemens. With the Cubs in a playoff chase, the emergence of the twenty-one-year-old seemed to be a dream come true for a franchise that had become, at best, lovable losers.

Six months later Kerry Wood lay on a table in Birmingham, Alabama, with his elbow swollen and wrapped in bandages. Instead of preparing for his first full season in the major leagues, Wood had undergone Tommy John surgery. Dr. James Andrews, the premier orthopedic surgeon in baseball, had replaced Wood's torn elbow ligaments with tendons cut from his hip. Wood's golden arm was now scarred, the triangular incision marking him as another of Andrews's many patients from all levels of baseball. Instead of throwing ninety-five miles an hour, Wood began a program that would take him more than a year to complete, finally returning to the Cubs lineup in 2000. A full season of a vaunted career was lost to rehab. The Cubs, a playoff team when Wood pitched, returned to the cellar of the National League.

In 2002 another young phenom entered the Cubs starting rotation with Wood. This one threw just as hard, pitched even better, and returned hope to a team that had had none since losing Wood to the surgeon's knife. Mark Prior was widely recognized as the greatest pitcher in collegiate history and rocketed to the major leagues after only two months in the minors. While the hopes of Cubs fans were buoyed, they remembered how years of Wood's promising career had been lost to injury. Prior, like most other young pitchers, would probably burn out, break down, and fade away. Most fans saw nothing different about him.

But Mark Prior *was* different. To the untrained eye he was just another pitcher, but from the age of sixteen Prior had been built to be different. While he wasn't a pure creation along the lines of Tiger Woods or the Williams sisters, his delivery had been built by Tom House, the former pitching coach of the Texas Rangers. Prior's biomechanical perfection stood out in stark contrast to Wood's splayed forearms and a follow through that ended with him falling toward first base.

Yet the story written large at the friendly confines of Wrigley Field hardly revealed the true reasons why these two similar pitchers ended their rookie seasons so differently. Wood was a high school phenom in Texas, often throwing both ends of a doubleheader. It wasn't unusual for him to throw as many as 150 pitches in a game. Scouts didn't see those numbers, and sportswriters certainly didn't monitor his workload, but inside the arm that was throwing schoolboy no-hitters, the damage was being done.

Mark Prior in a light workout.

While Wood was doing the damage that would end in surgery, Prior was faithfully performing mechanical drills assigned
to him by his team of coaches and trainers. After high school he
declined a professional baseball offer in favor of going to college, making him more mature when he did, inevitably, pitch in
the major leagues.

Despite the best efforts of modern thought and old-fashioned
teachings, pitching has always been more of an art, a battle of
craft versus violence. One man with nothing more than talent and
guile stands close enough to be killed if the sphere he throws is returned at him. Now, in seeking to analyze the act of pitching and
discovering ways to both prevent and correct injuries, we are

moving the art of pitching toward science. There is always more romance in art, but there is genius on both sides of this river.

Pitching is in a transition stage. We can break down a pitcher's mechanics in a BioDek, a machine that translates images of movement into simple drawings for analysis. We can repair a pitcher using the most advanced surgical techniques, and we can judge the results using sensitive cameras and lasers. Still, at the heart of it we have a man throwing a ball using fallible mechanics and, almost by definition, doing it to failure—to the point where he can no longer do so effectively. What causes this failure? It's simple fatigue, and when we learn how to measure this, we can stop relying on facile clichés or praying to the Lords of Baseball that Our Pitcher doesn't fall apart like we hope their pitcher does.

Pitching will always be art; analyzing the action and defense of the pitcher is science.

2

TAKING THE MOUND

Since a pitcher first threw a ball overhand—which did not happen until the twentieth century was bearing down on the nascent game of baseball—players have dealt with the knowledge that this form of throwing is not a natural act. The first pitching injury is unknown, lost to the mists of early baseball history, but the game itself protected its pitchers in those days.

Instead of being a game of high heat and inside fastballs, of power and deception, early baseball was truly pastoral and graceful. The pitcher was a sort of necessary evil, delivering the ball for a hitter who would then put the ball in play and set in motion the near-ballet of defense.

The pitcher in early ball games tossed the ball underhanded, more like a modern sidearmer than the traditional softball underhand. He was allowed a walking motion, which reduced the need for efficient mechanics.

But the greatest difference, one that lasted until the 1920s, was the ball. Modern fans take for granted the simple joy of catching a foul ball and taking it home with them. For each game the home team must supply several dozen brand-new white balls, readied by the plate umpire with a near ritualistic rubdown. Before 1921 most games were played with one ball. Some balls were used in more than one game and, as expected, would become soft and discolored. Worse, it was still legal to use foreign substances such as tobacco juice or slippery elm in order to throw an anti-spin pitch that is remembered as the spitball.

It took the 1920 beaning death of the Cleveland Indians' Roy Chapman to change the rules. This tragedy, in combination with an unruly young pitcher who carried a bat the size of a piano leg, prompted the era of modern pitching. While there were great pitchers before 1920, and plenty of them, comparing them with the pitchers of following years is near impossible.

How did Cy Young record 511 wins or throw 400 innings a year? The question always arises when modern pitch counts and innings limits are discussed. Simply put, early pitchers did not have to exert maximal effort on every pitch as modern pitchers do. In key situations or against the best hitter, a pitcher like Three Finger Brown or Christy Mathewson could pull out a fastball that would rival that of many modern pitchers, or go to a curve that, in Brown's case, had a motion described by an opposing hitter as "not subject to gravity until I've already swung, then all at once it remembers the laws."

But pitchers of the so-called Dead Ball Era before 1920 could be more efficient. They were throwing to batters who, instead of trying to hit the ball out of the park on every pitch, were often attempting just to put the ball in play and avoid striking out. Several players during the 1995–2003 "Explosive Era" struck out more in one season than Joe DiMaggio struck out in his entire career.

Some observers have bemoaned the lack of complete games in the modern era, using a "back in my day" argument that players aren't tough enough. Instead of appealing to machismo, these types are showing their ignorance of what in fact made those earlier pitchers successful. Allen Roth, a statistician employed by the Dodgers in the 1940s and 1950s, monitored pitch counts among other factors, and while data for the Dodgers and their opponents are far from as complete as one would wish for, the conclusion that players then were iron men, regularly racking up pitch counts that would break today's players, is simply not true. Instead they were regularly more efficient, completing games at 120 pitches and seldom venturing into the 130+ territory.

In the late 1950s and 1960s, some pitchers did begin to show a tolerance for higher pitch counts, but not in the general population. According to mathematical estimates from several sources, pitch counts on the whole rose only slightly while the great players like Juan Marichal and Sandy Koufax showed an ability that borders on masochistic. While Marichal's ability to absorb workload is amazing, Koufax left the game before his magical left arm left him completely. Sometimes abuse isn't measured by injury; it can often be measured best by lost opportunity.

If the maxim "Good pitching beats good hitting" is true, a good pitcher is a valuable resource and a great pitcher is gold to the men who fish the talent pool. It seems intuitive that these players would be guarded like bank vaults, coddled like high rollers in Vegas, and given more medical attention than a Munchausen case, but somehow they aren't. Trapped in a near-comical world of testosterone and machismo, history worshipping, and a "what have you done for me lately" mindset, pitchers are commodified and all too often wasted.

In the past five years there have been pitchers with the potential to be the next Juan Marichal, the next Sandy Koufax, or the next Kerry Wood. On playing fields in America and the world, these precious arms are being abused and the greatness wrung out of them like sweat. As great as the game is, it's almost sad how great the game could have been.

A pitcher is granted a save if he finishes a game with the lead in jeopardy and keeps the lead for his team. Pitchers like John Smoltz and Eric Gagne are paid handsomely for their skill in pitching one inning. While the statistic itself is somewhat overrated, the save is a statistic that should now be applied to those who manage the pitchers. For every pitcher who doesn't end up in an operating room, for every healthy arm that's kept in an organization, we should be granting a save of sorts to the coaches, minor league directors, and front offices of baseball.

The tools to save pitchers and to change the game of baseball are available. In this book we have collected the best modern thinking about pitching, pitcher abuse, and pitcher health. Our hope is that we will share in a game where pitcher injuries are a thing of the past.

Hitting Them in the Pocketbook

Appealing to the Lords of Baseball through vague notions like "the good of the game" is something akin to asking a pig not to roll in fresh mud. Perhaps a better analogy would be asking the owners not to save a nickel. Often it is only when the owner of a team is paying out millions of dollars to a pitcher who is rehabbing from surgery that the question arises how that pitcher ended up there in the first place.

In the last round of negotiations between the owners and the players' union, the game came within hours of grinding to a halt over what amounted to a difference of $500 million over the period of the agreement. While this dollar figure is not a

Tom House talks to young players about pitching mechanics.

small matter, and while the agreement was eventually made, there would have been one simple way to give owners both the cost savings they demanded while taking nothing away from the players: reducing injuries.

Over the period covered by the agreement, the owners can expect to pay out nearly a billion dollars in expenses for injured players (not all of them pitchers, of course). This figure includes salaries paid to players unable to perform, medical expenses, insurance costs, lost revenue, and the cost of replacement players. Not included in this total is opportunity lost. When a player goes down to injury, the team is left without a player who was counted on to provide service. The more irreplaceable the player, the more the team will suffer—and it follows that the highest-paid players are often the most irreplaceable.

The Los Angeles Dodgers are one of the more storied franchises in baseball, but in the example that follows they are no different from the other twenty-nine major league teams. They contract with players at market prices in return for their exclusive services. The Dodgers, in 1993, had the second overall pick in the amateur draft. Feeling a need, General Manager Fred Claire selected a college closer named Darren Dreifort from Wichita State with the second overall pick. The Dodgers chose Dreifort just behind Alex Rodriguez and ahead of such future major league pitchers as Brian Anderson and Billy Wagner. By the following season, Dreifort was in Dodger Stadium.

With every pitch, while Dodger fans thought they saw the next great pitcher in their rich history, Dreifort was doing damage. His mechanics were violent, and his elbow absorbed most of the force of his delivery. Pitching in only twenty-seven games in 1994, Dreifort's elbow finally gave out. Dr. Frank Jobe, the inventor of Tommy John surgery, had another client, and Dreifort soon had a new elbow ligament.

It would be easy to blame the Dodgers for Dreifort's injury, but the damage in his elbow was cumulative. It wasn't the last twenty-nine innings he pitched that caused it; the injury was near inevitable. If anything, the Dodgers can only be blamed for not doing more to prevent the injury or, more likely, for placing their hopes on a pitcher whose mechanics were unsound. Could—or should—the Dodgers have known better? Certainly there were warning signs. According to one scout who watched Dreifort in college, "You knew he wasn't going to last. He was a closer in Wichita because he wouldn't have held up."

After Tommy John surgery, Dreifort returned to pitch in mid-season of 1996. For the 1996 and 1997 seasons he pitched in relief and showed the same form that made the hearts of both scouts and fans race—and that led Dreifort to Frank Jobe's operating table. Despite his ability to pitch again, the damage had

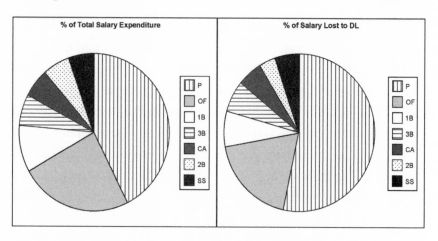

begun again. It was accelerated by a decision to move Dreifort into the starting rotation in 1998. This decision actually seemed to work, allowing Dreifort to complete almost three and a half seasons without significant injury, but with each pitch—like any pitcher—Dreifort was closer and closer to seeing his elbow break down again.

It might be expected that the Dodgers and their medical team knew Dreifort better than anyone else and would therefore know the risks inherent in his pitching motion. Somehow that knowledge didn't make it upstairs, and in 2000 Dreifort was signed to a long-term contract for more than $50 million.

It is one thing to lose $250,000 or so, the amount the Dodgers paid Dreifort while he recovered from Tommy John surgery over the course of three seasons. It's quite another thing to lose $30 million to the same injury. Just half a season into his big new contract, Dreifort once again headed for surgery. He returned in 2003 but survived only half a season before another injury—this time to his knee, requiring experimental surgery—put him back on the shelf. His return is unknown, but he is owed $24 million for the next two seasons.

I don't mean to pick on either Dreifort or the Dodgers, but they serve as an example for the industry. Pitcher injuries are often predictable, and the costs of these injuries are exacerbated by excessive contracts made without complete information.

The San Francisco Giants are a team without unlimited funds, just like every team not located in the Bronx. In order to reduce the loss of payroll "flexibility"—a buzzword in modern baseball—the Giants decided to both empower and hold accountable their medical staff. According to their athletic trainer, Stan Conte, "All personnel decisions come to my desk. I have to put my name on the line and say that I think this guy or that guy is a good or bad risk. It's just one of the factors that Brian [Sabean, the Giants general manager] uses when he's making decisions. But if I'm wrong, they know exactly where I am."

Few teams take the Giants' enlightened approach to accountability. Too many teams see injury as "part of the game" or predestined. For every dollar they spend on rehab, they spend less than a dime on prevention. Few of the thirty baseball owners earned the money they have by making such ignorant and shortsighted business decisions.

While pitching injuries can probably never be eliminated (though it's possible), a fractional reduction in the number and severity of these injuries would result in a savings significantly greater than what the players and owners fought over in 2002. Add the amplification of talent that would result and the decision to do what the Giants did seems a no-brainer. Somehow, in baseball, it isn't.

The Front Lines

Very little notice is paid to most members of a major league medical staff. Some are stars who transcend their peers, as among players, but most are well-qualified, hardworking men (and occasionally women) who make up the first line of defense for pitchers. Working in concert, ideally, with the manager, the pitching coach, the general manager, and various assistants as well as team doctors, physical therapists, nutritionists, and strength coaches, the athletic trainers are the foot soldiers in the battle to keep pitchers healthy.

These trained medical personnel are often overlooked by the media. When a player is injured, in all but a few cases the media will pepper the manager with questions. At best the manager can parrot the information given to him by the trainers or team physicians, but most often his ability to translate the information is poor. Some exchanges are merely unhelpful; others are laughable or pathetic. In my experience covering the daily operations of baseball injuries, I have never once learned anything about an injury from a manager.

Trainers—usually a staff of two, but expansion to three is becoming more common—often work twelve-hour days or longer. I have called trainers at 6 a.m. to find them already working with players, and I have called trainers after midnight when they are often still in their facilities, working with players after a game. With the long hours, travel, and pressure, many of these men sacrifice much, if not all, of their social or family lives. Comparatively they are poorly paid. "I once asked if I could get a percentage of the money I saved the team," one trainer told me. "They didn't go for it." Small wonder. Ten percent of a 10 percent reduction from the average dollars lost would net that trainer well over a million dollars. The average pay for a trainer in 2002, the last year data was available, was under $100,000.

The medical staff of a baseball team has grown up from the days when a poorly trained man who was little more than a glorified clubby would become the team's trainer. In the late 1920s, men with nicknames like "Bonesetter" and "Saw-bones" would try to "milk" the swelling out of joints, rub down players with salves of capsicum (the substance that makes peppers hot), and put them in tubs of ice. There was lit-tle if any science to the process.

Today the trainer often has a graduate degree and is certi-fied by the National Athletic Training Association after a series of grueling exams. He will average twenty-two years of experi-ence. He will supervise another trainer, also degreed, certified, and fully capable. Trainers have copious amounts of medical equipment at their disposal. From simple tape to complex elec-trical and ultrasound modalities, from underwater treadmills and therapy tubs to medical closets that look like a combina-tion of health food store and pharmacy, trainers are given all the tools.

Trainers are in a strange position. While they are in charge of the day-to-day management of player health, they are also technically subservient to the team physicians. Many training rooms post the doctor's "standing orders" on the wall to give their authority a public platform. While most trainers have a good relationship with their team physicians, opposing views sometimes cause problems. Add in the liberal use of consulting physicians, especially in orthopedic cases, and the trainer may be placed in awkward positions.

The trainer is also asked to work with associated health pro-fessionals. Most teams will have a physical therapist on staff or in close association with the club, as well as a strength and con-ditioning coach. Many modern players also have a variety of personal staff, from nutritionists to yoga instructors. In the middle of this cluster is often the overworked, underpaid trainer.

At the top of his profession is a man who understands the demands of the job like no one else, the Giants' head trainer Stan Conte. Conte is responsible not only for a normal team of twenty-five players but for one particular player who is more closely watched than any: Barry Bonds. Because of Bonds's advancing age and problems with his hamstrings, it has often fallen to Conte to keep Bonds and his prodigious power in the lineup over the past three record-breaking seasons. With his former assistant, Barney Nugent, Conte regularly places the Giants at the top of lists in fewest days and dollars lost to the Disabled List.

Conte is a strong, imposing presence and has been called both abrasive and impressive by colleagues. While he has the near universal respect of his peers, he also realizes that he is not well liked. "No one likes the guy in front of them," he said one day, standing on the field as the Giants took batting practice. "I've been in front for a while, and no one wants to be held accountable." Conte is a certified athletic trainer, but he came to the profession in something of a roundabout way. He originally worked as a physical therapist and then came to the Giants as their strength and conditioning coach.

After taking over as head athletic trainer in 2000, he was able to take charge of a medical program that he had begun to revolutionize three years earlier. "We made a decision to reduce injuries," he said. "Sometimes it was simple, like making sure our athletes talked to us and the coaches understood where we were coming from [as a medical staff]. In other cases it was looking at things a bit differently than we or anyone had.

"One of the most innovative things we did was our sprints. Everyone does those, right? All year long, from the first day of spring training to [daily] warm-ups. We watched everyone running and—I don't remember who it was—someone said that no player ever runs straight for that far a distance. It's all left turns, like a race car.

"I started asking people why we ran sprints, and the answer was always 'because we always have.' I wasn't satisfied with that. We began running our sixty-yard sprint with a turn, just like the player would going from first to third or second to home. Adding that specific not only made sense—since it was something these guys actually do in game—it helped reduce our injuries. We started seeing a reduction in hamstring injuries almost instantly."

Conte's grasp of seemingly obvious yet innovative solutions is just one way he distinguishes himself. His holistic understanding of conditioning, rehabilitation, and therapy gives him a unique perspective. He is also deeply indebted to his former assistant, Barney Nugent. While Conte can be imposing, Nugent is the kind of guy you'd expect to see on the barstool next to you. With a thick New England accent and a quick smile, Nugent gave no indication that he was in as much pain as his patients during the 2003 season. Suffering from symptoms of myasthenia gravis, Nugent fought through the season and never let it slow him down.

"I worked with Ray Durham [the Giants' second baseman who suffers from chronic leg problems] so much that I felt like we were going steady," he said laughing. "I'd be in here early with him, and then I'd be in here late with him. When I finally got him ready, I walked up to him and said 'Ray, we gotta break up now'—and we both laughed." Nugent retired after the 2003 season; Conte will be hard-pressed to replace him.

The Giants' most famous player, Barry Bonds, often works with his own staff of nutritionists, coaches, and doctors. Asked how he dealt with the added personalities and potentially conflicting programs, Conte said, "Sometimes you have to let Barry be Barry. He obviously knows what he's doing. It's a matter of education and communication. We set up a program that had flexibility to do what he needed to do. If it wasn't working—and it's hard to say that when you look at what he's done—we would have had to take another look at it."

Conte also is a proponent of education in one of the more explosive issues in baseball, the use of dietary supplements. "We bring them in and look at what they're taking. We have to have a certain level of trust—they can talk and not be judged. Sometimes they're taking ten things and five of them have the same ingredients, or a couple of them cancel each other out. None of these guys has a degree in chemistry, and sometimes they get bad advice. What works for the guy in the next locker might not work for him."

While Conte and the Giants take a pro-active approach to player health, across the bay the Oakland Athletics have taken pro-active to a whole new level, even inventing a new word to define it: prehab. Pitching coach Rick Peterson (who has now left the A's for a similar position with the New York Mets) worked closely with Dr. Glenn Fleisig of the American Sports Medicine Institute (ASMI) over a period of years to develop a philosophy that was called by another pitching coach "equal parts science and voodoo." But in a game where nearly everything is measured, Peterson's prehab program has unassailable results. In the past two seasons the A's have not only had no pitching-arm injuries at the major league level, they have had only one minor pitching-arm injury in their entire system.

While Michael Lewis chronicled the A's system extensively in his best-selling book *Moneyball*, there was little coverage of the A's pitching. Some of Lewis's critics have argued that he ignored their pitching since the A's trio of starters—Barry Zito, Tim Hudson, and Mark Mulder—did not fit his thesis about how the A's put a team together. I don't believe this. When I asked Lewis what stories he covered but didn't include, he immediately turned to Hudson and Zito. "I thought Hudson was going to be a very important character," Lewis told me, "but it just didn't fit in. Like any book, some things are left on the cutting-room floor." As for Zito, his colorful nature might have distracted readers from the message of the book. "I could write a whole book about Zito," Lewis said, "but it's not this book."

While *Moneyball* focused on the front office and what Lewis called an "island of misfit toys" roster, the A's are blessed with a top-notch pitching staff that is as good or better than any competing team at significantly lower prices. Including three of the best young starting pitchers in the game, this rotation gives the A's a significant advantage. But like any young rotation, they are sure to experience health problems. Among this trio, Mark Mulder has been most injury prone, with back problems in 2001 and a fractured hip in 2003. Again, it is important to note that neither of these injuries involves the pitching arm. Mulder's hip injury was pitching related in that a substandard mound damaged his hip, but this injury was hardly the fault of the A's prehab program.

In an interview with Jonah Keri, Peterson described some of his techniques, which include sensory deprivation drills, personality testing, and rhythmic pitching in addition to the normal and scientifically derived pitching fundamentals. Peterson's work with Dr. Fleisig has given the A's and ASMI an incredible amount of data to work with, certainly an advantage over other teams. Others, like the Boston Red Sox and the Cleveland Indians, have also begun work with ASMI, and with Peterson's move to the Mets there is little doubt that his techniques will move with him. (We'll discuss this work in more detail later.)

Pitching with the eyes closed might seem like something out of *Zen and the Art of Motorcycle Maintenance*, but Peterson believes it to be a tool that makes sense in developing pitchers. "We do a lot of work with guys early in their careers with their eyes closed," he says, "just training the body to move efficiently. We'll deprive them of sound, or add sound like loud music so they can get a feel for working under those conditions."

In the quest to save pitchers from injury, these and many other trainers and coaches are doing amazing, forward-thinking work in multiple disciplines. From biometrics and biomechanics to new surgical techniques to coaches who seek to advance their knowledge in order to gain an advantage and to make baseball a better game, no field is doing as much good while being held back by what can best be called an entrenched old-boy network.

Anyone who is in danger of losing his job—in this case frequently the only profession these baseball men have known—will react strongly against something new and different, something few of them understand and others lack the means to integrate. The vast majority of pitching coaches today were once pitchers themselves; they pass along the anecdotal knowledge they have picked up in their years in the game. I cannot argue that many of them are fine coaches and have a great deal of wisdom to impart, but if these men are not overtaken by a new breed of coach, personified by Rick Peterson or the disciples of Tom House or Mike Marshall, the game will have failed and we will have failed to save the pitchers.

3

FROM COLISEUM TO ARENA
A Historical Note on
Sports Medicine

(with thanks to Dr. William Carroll, University of Mobile)

Athletic training, in its various forms, is almost as old as recorded history. The first "athletic trainer" was probably Herodicus, who cared for the health of the Roman gladiators in the fifth century B.C. Although he was officially classified as a physician, he was the first recorded health-care provider to advocate physical medicine as both a preventative and a curative. One of his more famous student apprentices was Hippocrates, recognized as the father of medicine. To this day, athletic trainers like to point out to physicians that Hippocrates was taught by an athletic trainer.

With the fall of the Roman Empire, athletic trainers disappear from recorded history. We can find mentions only of individuals working with the sport of boxing who were adept at massage techniques and highly secretive about the formulas of their liniment-type solutions. At the beginning of the twentieth century, professional baseball and fledgling collegiate football programs provided opportunities for individuals to care for those athletes, and they were called trainers. With nicknames like Bonesetter and Sawbones, these individuals often had little formal education in their field because very little existed at the time.

Instead they were schooled in apprenticeships with physicians or trainers already working in the field. Although they often lacked an education in the background sciences of anatomy and physiology, they made up for their lack of scientific background by dedicating themselves to the "arts" of athletic training, which at that time consisted primarily of massage and taping. Many of the early texts in athletic training devoted themselves almost exclusively to the art of "strapping," or what we today call taping. Early trainers are said to have claimed "they could tape anything but the crack of dawn and broken hearts."

The profession of athletic training has always been closely aligned with physicians. In the early years of the twentieth century, it was a physician, Dr. S. E. Bilik of Bellevue Hospital in New York City, who truly inaugurated the evolution of athletic training from an art to a profession. Dr. Bilik was keenly interested in sports and in the athletes who participated in them. He recognized that if more appropriately trained individuals were available to care for athletes on a daily basis, many injuries could be prevented or their seriousness minimized.

In pursuit of this goal, Dr. Bilik held numerous training sessions for early athletic health-care providers and in 1917 published what is recognized as the first athletic training education text, *The Athletic Trainer's Bible*. In recognition of his efforts on behalf of the profession, in 1962 Dr. Bilik was inducted into the National Athletic Trainers Association Hall of Fame.

The Cramer Chemical Company of Gardner, Kansas, was a founding sponsor of the National Athletic Trainers Association and in 1950 underwrote the first NATA convention. The founders of the company, Chuck and Frank Cramer, supported the athletic training profession throughout their lives; their company remains a major supplier of athletic training supplies and equipment. Its success can be traced to an ankle injury suffered by Chuck Cramer in 1912 when he was a track and field athlete at the University of Kansas. Cramer used his knowledge of chemistry to concoct a liniment to treat his injury, and he continued to compete. That liniment was the first product of the fledgling chemical company when it opened for business in 1918; its first customers were the practicing athletic trainers of the day.

In a step aimed at advancing the field of athletic training and providing a measure of recognition, the Cramer Company published a monthly newsletter, the "First Aider" that was sent not only to all practicing athletic trainers but to every college and high school in the United States. It also sponsored Cramer Student Trainer Clinics throughout the country to provide basic skills to these high school and college students who, at the time, were often the only available caregivers for the athletes at their schools since not all schools had a full-time athletic trainer on staff.

Professional baseball provided a strong base of athletic trainers from the 1920s to the 1940s, at a time when very few colleges or other professional sports teams recognized the benefits of having an athletic trainer on the payroll. Still, these people had little or no medical background, and there was no system of training the trainers. In an age when baseball was remaking itself on the field, it was not yet ready to do so in the training room.

Throughout this period, athletic trainers also lacked an organizational structure. They were individuals whose worth was not widely recognized in the world of sports. There was no vehicle in place for the sharing of information, no criteria for entering the field, and certainly no public relations activities in their behalf. An attempt to form such an organization was made by a group of athletic trainers at the Drake Relays in the late 1940s, but their efforts were quickly thwarted by collegiate athletic administrators who feared that the trainers were trying to form a union.

If one had to identify the major events that moved athletic training toward recognition as a profession, those events would undoubtedly be the formation of the National Athletic Trainers Association and the first NATA convention in 1950. This gathering of approximately two hundred athletic training practitioners provided a means for the sharing of information, the promotion of athletic training as a viable entity, and the advancement to professionalism.

Some of these hardworking founding fathers of the NATA included Spike Dixon of Indiana University (author of the *Dixonary of Athletic Training Techniques*), Pinky Newell of Purdue University, Ducky Drake of UCLA, Eddie Wojecki of Rice University, Tom Sheehan of Rensselaer Polytechnic Institute, Billy Fallon of the Naval Academy, and Kenny Howard of Auburn University. Professional baseball trainers who were unable to attend the convention (because their teams were competing at the time) but who were instrumental in the birth of NATA included Walter Bakke and Gene Geiselman, both of the St. Louis Cardinals, Bob Bauman of St. Louis University and the Cleveland Browns, Charles "Doc" Turner of the Negro National League (and the Harlem Globetrotters), Eugene Harvey of the Brooklyn Dodgers, and Frank Wiechec of the Phillies.

Building on the momentum of that first NATA convention, athletic trainers took strides toward building the profession.

They now had a structure and a colloquium through which to exchange ideas, learn from one another, and determine their professional weaknesses and take steps to eliminate them. Their relationship with physicians, with whom they had always worked fairly closely, became more formal. Physicians became keynote speakers not only at the national NATA convention but also at regional and local sports medicine seminars. This enhanced relationship brought a deepening of respect between the two groups.

In a landmark pronouncement in 1961, athletic training was recognized as a profession by the American Medical Association. This recognition brought on new responsibilities: there had to be a way of ensuring that those who called themselves athletic trainers actually possessed the requisite education and clinical experience to perform in the profession. Toward this end, the National Athletic Trainers Association took steps to develop national certification criteria for athletic trainers.

As it evolved, this certification required, first, a college degree with certain required courses, and fifteen hundred hours of supervised clinical experience. It also required the aspiring athletic trainer to pass a three-part national examination consisting of a written test, a simulated test of competencies and knowledge, and an oral practical test. Until an individual had passed all three parts of this exam, he could not be a Certified Athletic Trainer by NATA's Board of Certification (now referred to as a NATABOC Certified Athletic Trainer). The first national certification exam was given in 1969.

Athletic training in professional baseball responded to changes in the profession. The Major League Players Association worked to develop a clause in the Collective Bargaining Agreement that required all trainers working in professional baseball to be NATABOC Certified. It was also during this time, in 1973, that the Professional Baseball Athletic Trainers Society (PBATS) was formed. This group not only assured a uniformity of athletic health care for professional baseball players at all levels, it also pushed for educational programs for its members beyond those required by the NATA. PBATS conducts an annual meeting before the beginning of spring training to discuss athletic health-care issues as they pertain to professional baseball and provides an educational forum for its members. Under the leadership of outstanding NATABOC Certified Athletic Trainers, this organization has helped bring professional baseball health care from the days of liniment and tape to the scientifically based injury prevention and rehabilitation profession of today.

The latest evolution in the professionalization of athletic training has involved education. At one time athletic training education was virtually on-the-job training. Today, under the guidance of the National Athletic Trainers Association, the NATA Education Council, and the Joint Review Commission for Athletic Training, educational programs in the field have become strongly scientifically based, with balanced classroom and clinical education. Effective January 1, 2004, all athletic training education programs must be accredited.

Outstanding athletic training educators such as Herb Amato of George Mason University, Dr. Sue Shapiro of Barry University in Miami, Tom Weidner of Ball State University, and Pete Koehneke of Canisius College have worked diligently to professionalize and standardize athletic training education. PBATS has also been a major contributor to athletic training clinical education by providing internships for athletic training students.

The next time you see an athletic trainer on the job, whether at a major league baseball game, a collegiate or high school game, or in a sports medicine clinic, be aware that this individual is a highly trained professional, educated and experienced, who works long hours to assure that the athletes or other physically active people in his or her care receive the best possible attention.

4

THE FUNCTIONAL ANATOMY OF PITCHING

In discussing the anatomical and biomechanical aspects of pitching, the focus is often on the dominant arm because it is so apparent in the process. Some phrases like "golden arm" and "million-dollar arm" have become part of the game. In looking at a pitcher, however, the arm is not the be-all and end-all of success or failure.

Neither are the legs, in contrast to the "drop and drive" theory that followed on the heels of Tom Seaver's successful career. His style became a teaching point based on a singular success. While the legs are certainly an important point, looking at Seaver's or Prior's calves, or the massive thighs of Roger Clemens, gives us little insight into what makes a pitcher successful.

But there is one key piece of data, one part of the pitcher's anatomy that cannot be out of whack and still allow for success. It is also the reason that a pitcher who looks less like a prototype and more like . . . well, like an average guy or a skinny Dominican can have the success that Billy Wagner or Pedro Martinez have. The one key piece of information, the one talent that every successful pitcher at any level has is the ability to accelerate the hips. Quick: name one drill that teaches this or that seeks to improve this skill. Most pitching coaches I posed this problem to came up blank. That, in a nutshell, is one of the major reasons why at every level we are often failing our pitchers.

As important as the hips are, it is more important to remember that pitching is a process. No matter how much inherent talent a pitcher may have through genetics, poor mechanics will either reduce that gift or force it to be lost to injury. A simple definition of pitching is also a lesson in the anatomy of pitching: the act of throwing a ball by generating force with the lower body that is carried through in a natural line by the pitching arm. Let's break this down by components, working our way along the natural path of force creation.

Legs

"How's he supposed to be a good pitcher? His ass isn't nearly big enough. I want a guy with a fat ass, like Clemens." So said Bill "Spaceman" Lee, on seeing Carl Pavano pitch in Montreal.

The prototype pitcher has big legs. Looking at pitchers like Prior or Clemens, one cannot help but notice the sheer mass of their legs. Prior's calves are as big as some men's thighs. Clemens, as the Spaceman pointed out, does have some features in common with Jennifer Lopez. In 2003 Dontrelle Willis burst on the major league scene with solid performances and a leg kick that was made for marketing. With his eyes rolling, Willis brings his front leg up, and at times his foot comes level with his eyes.

What function do the legs have in the proper pitching delivery? They serve as the beginning of the drive to the plate, they function as part of the timing mechanism, and they are a key to maintaining what Tom House calls "dynamic balance."

Dynamic balance is defined as the maintenance of balance in relation to a shifting center of gravity throughout the whole of a pitching motion. Young pitchers especially have a problem with balance, and their pitching motion is often little more than a poorly controlled fall in the general direction of the batter.

While there are extremes in relation to the leg lift of pitchers —from the high kick of Dontrelle Willis or Nolan Ryan to the

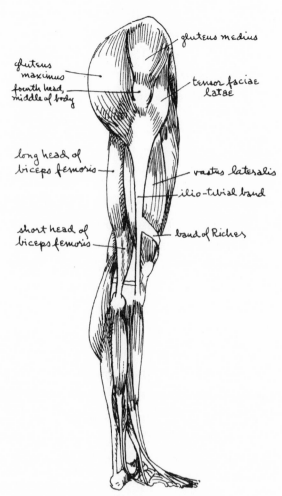

The leg and hip, schematic drawing.

near slide-step of Greg Maddux or Robb Nen—as long as there is balance and consistency, there is little advantage to be gained in adjustments. If a pitcher is comfortable and balanced throughout, the leg kick shouldn't be adjusted. Proof of this comes in the slide-step, the adjustment made to alter the pitcher's look and timing when a potential base stealer is on first. Pitchers tend to lose very little in the way of control or velocity when the slide-step is used sparingly.

The second key is keeping the hamstrings and groin flexible and strong. We'll cover this in more detail later, but as with any base or foundation, a breakdown here will always affect a pitcher adversely, even if the injury is minor. Worse, hamstring and groin injuries tend to become chronic or cascading.

Hips

While most coaches would focus on the arms or the legs, it is in fact the hips that are the most important part of the pitching motion. Within the kinetic chain of pitching, the rotation of the hips imparts the most energy to the ball. According to Dr. Mike Marshall, the pitcher should "maximize the rotational distance over which they apply force. Also, just as ice skaters spin faster when they stand tall, pitchers rotate faster, which generates greater force. As viewed from above, while pitchers rotate about the axis of their body, they apply force straight toward home plate with their pitching arm."

In fact, hip rotational velocity is more closely associated with pitch velocity than any other mechanism in the chain. According to research done by Dr. Glenn Fleisig, which looked at the force generation of many pitchers during biomechanical analysis, most of the force was generated at or near the hips.

"Eighty percent of power is created at the core," says Rick Peterson, "from the top of the knee to the bottom of the ribcage."

This force is directly related to both the strength and flexibility of the hips. This lack of understanding of the biomechanics of pitching holds back most pitching coaches and prevents them from enhancing the motions of their pitchers. In a survey of sixty-five high school coaches, only one did any sort of drill that focused on hip rotation.

Pitching coaches often also fail to address the need to keep the hips—notably the hip flexor muscles—both strong and flexible. Without strength through the entire needed range of motion, a pitcher is unable to generate his maximal velocity.

Back

Second only to the shoulder as a source of injuries is the lower back. The spine and its supporting muscles are extremely important to the delivery of the ball since they are the connecting, bracing element that must carry much of the potential force from the hips and legs through the body to the arm.

Thinking of the chain like a whip—a metaphor used for hitting by Chris Yeager, a top hitting coach—is an accurate way to approach it. The back is that unexciting portion of the whip that carries the wave of energy between handle and tip—never noticed unless it fails.

The typical back problem is muscular, but continued trauma to the area, or one powerful incident of trauma, can produce herniation of the intravertebral discs. While injuries to that series of muscles than supports the spine are serious, they are no different that any other muscle. Only significant tearing will cause more than soreness and spasm. The spasm is often

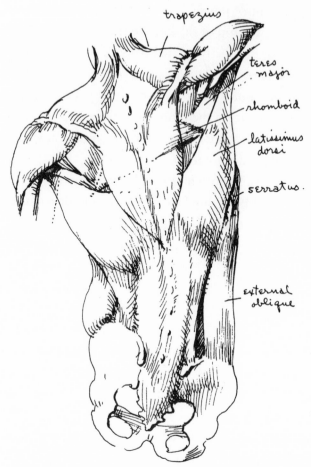

The back, schematic drawing.

sufficient to bring a player out of a game, but more than half the time the spasm can be treated effectively with therapeutic agents and medication, bringing the athlete back to competition with little or no loss of time.

A herniation, however, is of the utmost concern to a pitcher. While a hitter can overcome a minor herniation with a trunk-strengthening program or minimally invasive surgery, a pitcher puts so much stress on the lower back with every pitch, proper mechanics or not, that being able to pitch effectively with this type of injury is extremely difficult. Severe herniations can be career ending.

"Core strengthening" is a suddenly popular term that simply means a series of strength and flexibility exercises that build up the spinal erectors, the abdominals, and the obliques. These muscles support the spine and keep it from hyperflexing or hyperextending, both of which put immense and traumatic pressure on the ligaments of the spinal column and the intravertebral discs.

Of all the various areas of the body, only the spine and its supporting structure of muscles and ligaments is damaged by flexibility. No one wants to be accused of "lacking backbone." That logic also dictates that a floppy, flexible spine is not a positive. Of course one needs a degree of flexibility and mobility in order to perform athletic and daily activities. Moderation, the Dalai Lama tells us, and in this, rigidity is as bad as too much mobility.

The abdominals are key to good spinal health and posture. In baseball terms, a fat pitcher with a belly that hangs over his belt is putting more baseline stress on the spine because of his extra weight and the lack of tone in his abs to support and counteract the spinal erectors.

A great pitcher needs a strong trunk as a solid part of the kinetic chain, transferring the energy forward from the push of the ground and better than halfway toward the ball exploding out of his hand.

Shoulder

The average man or woman on the street, if asked, would say that the shoulder is both the focus of, generation point for, and

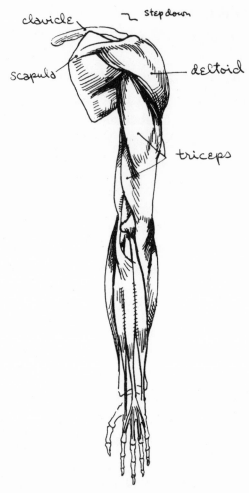

The shoulder and arm, schematic drawing.

most injured part of the pitching anatomy. We have already established that it is not the first two, but it surprises many to find that the shoulder is not the most often injured.

The shoulder is a complex joint, surrounding a ball-and-socket insertion of the humerus (the bone of the upper arm) into the glenoid fossa. This connection is cushioned and aided by the glenoid labrum and surrounded by a capsule. The shoulder is primarily moved by the deltoids, and the rotator cuff is responsible for deceleration and structural stability.

There is a simple "medhead" generality in regard to arm injuries: the shoulder is velocity, the elbow is control. Without other explanation, a drop in velocity most likely indicates a shoulder injury such as a torn rotator cuff, a cuff impingement, or tendonitis.

Pitchers often describe injuries to their rotator cuffs as "paper tearing." When overtaxed and overextended, the fibers of the rotator cuff will, as with any muscle, tear. Every improper or overloaded pitch produces muscular trauma on a micro level. Given a specific or cumulative stress, these fibers give way in a pattern that may involve anything from a minor strain to a full thickness tear.

The work of Dr. Frank Jobe to develop specific exercises and training to help strengthen and prevent rotator cuff injuries has been among the more successful medical interventions. While full thickness tears of the cuff are increasingly rare, there has been a recent increase in the overuse injuries of labrum tears and tendonitis.

There is a simple way to reduce overuse injuries of the shoulder: reduce workload. Unfortunately the state of the game does not allow for simple medhead logic to win the day. Instead teams ideally want to find a balance between maximum effective use of their pitching asset and minimum loss of function for that same asset. Finding a balance—in essence, tiptoeing on a line between health and functionality—is the difficult task that must be accomplished by the combined efforts of the pitcher, his coaches, and the medical staff.

Modern pitchers have injuries in the natural swelling of the shoulder. Taken to an extreme, it can cause both significant pain, soreness, and friction damage. As a tendon is stressed or irritated, it swells, just as any other tissue in the body does as a defense. This pain and swelling is the body's signal to discontinue the activity until the body part returns to normal. Through pain tolerance, modern therapy, and painkillers, many athletes override this natural instinct and continue the very activity that put them into pain. There begins a vicious cycle of overuse, pain, treatment, and quick return to use.

If the pain signal is going to be overridden—and here we must distinguish clearly between normal muscular soreness and pain—care must be taken to prevent further damage from occurring in the use cycle, and to treat or maintain the level of the injury. Pitchers can pitch when sore. Some can even tolerate significant levels of pain, well above what "normal humans" are willing to tolerate in search of further excellence in their sport. In numerous studies, elite athletes have been found to have few common traits beyond a high pain tolerance.

Impingement can be treated with anti-inflammatory medication, therapeutic agents, and, if necessary, surgery. Surgery in these cases is a clear last resort, despite positive prognosis, due to the time lost to recovery and rehab. A procedure known as a modified Mumford is showing great promise. A small section at the end of the clavicle is removed, allowing a larger space for the bicipital tendon and relieving the pressure caused by the inflammation. Face it: pushing a three-inch ball through a two-inch hole might amuse a toddler, but it's bad news for a pitcher. The swollen tendon does not move smoothly through its naturally allotted space.

Recently more pitchers are being diagnosed with a tear to the glenoid labrum. The labrum is a cartilage mesh like the knee's meniscus. The labrum cannot only tear but may also detach. Jim Palmer, the Hall of Fame pitcher, has observed that modern players see more labrum tears because of enhanced imaging tools. This may be true, but probably it is more likely that pitchers from past eras suffered labrum tears and were let go, ending what may have been promising careers.

Jay Jaffe, a New York–based sportswriter, tells what it was like to go through labrum surgery in the fall of 2003.

> . . . Yours truly has been playing hurt since mid-June. In a horseplay-related swimming pool accident—exactly the kind your mother warned you about—I injured my right shoulder. Hanging out at my pal Nick's parents' place in Northampton, Massachusetts, I agreed, in my infinite wisdom, to some competitive tomfoolery which involved me diving onto a flotation mat. Genius. My hands instinctively went out to cushion my landing, but my right hand slipped and slid sideways across the mat, pinning my elbow in the vicinity of my sternum and sending a sickening jolt of pain through my shoulder.
>
> The short version is that I tore my labrum, and after three months of physical therapy that haven't solved the problem, I'm slated to undergo arthroscopic surgery on Wednesday, November 19, to repair the damage. I've spent the last two weeks shuttling back and forth between doctors and labs, getting all of my ducks in a row in preparation for this. I've been stuck with needles so many times I feel like a human pincushion, but I guess that's good practice for what will happen next week.
>
> The *labrum* is a ring of fibrous cartilage that surrounds the end of the scapula (the shoulder blade) and holds the head of the humerus (the upper arm bone) as a ball-and-socket joint. My magnetic resonance scans (MRI), which weren't done until about a month after the injury, showed that I sustained a common type of tear called a *SLAP tear*.

In addition to being something I'm tempted to do to myself every time I explain my injury, SLAP stands for Superior Labral Anterior Posterior. Basically, the lining of my shoulder joint was torn front to back.

Following the diagnosis by my orthopedic surgeon, I went through three months of physical therapy, which did help some in alleviating the impingement syndrome from which I suffered. But even now, my shoulder is still unstable, I've been unable to return to anything approaching my normal regimen of lifting weights, and many of my daily activities, such as opening windows and doors or holding onto a railing on the subway, cause me pain. I wake up several times each night to reposition my arm. I haven't thrown a baseball since a couple of hours after sustaining the injury, which I attempted for diagnostic purposes, finding that even flipping the ball twenty feet was a chore. Basically, my shoulder felt as though it had the wind knocked out of it, and though I can't point to a single specific area that's sore, getting through a day pain-free is like trying to cover for an unfilled cavity—sooner or later I do something to remind myself just how much I hurt.

My doctors and every other reliable source of information I've consulted have been pretty unanimous that at this stage the shoulder isn't going to get any better by itself, and that the surgery, which is 85–95 percent successful, is about as minimal as it gets. Basically, I'll be put out via general anesthesia and given a nerve block via a shot to my neck (mmmmm). Three incisions about a centimeter in diameter will be made in my shoulder, one in the back and two in the front. Using an arthroscope, a narrow fiber optic instrument with a camera, they'll peek into the joint through the incisions. They'll check my rotator cuff, which by most indications is probably normal, and reattach my labrum to the scapula via suture anchors. This kind of surgery is an outpatient procedure, so I'll be going home the same day, and after a few days of convalescing, I should be able to work the following week.

It's the rehab which is a bitch. To give my shoulder time to heal, I can't do much of anything for the first four weeks beyond the simple things—feeding myself, typing, and some light range-of-motion stuff. So long, ski season. After that I'm looking at about four and a half to six months before I can resume full activity, including breaking out my mitt to toss the ol' horsehide around. That feels like an eternity right now, but it's a better outlook than chronic pain and a throwing motion my girlfriend wouldn't sign for (she can zing it).

It's a good thing my baseball career is limited to the occasional game of catch or a rare turn in the batting cage, because a torn labrum is something no ballplayer wants to mess with.

Jaffe is right about that. SLAP lesions are one of the "big five" injuries that cause nearly half of all lost playing time. Technically the anatomical structure that makes the SLAP lesion possible is the origin of the tendon of the long head of the biceps muscle and the way it hooks over the head of the humerus. If the arm is forcibly bent inward at the shoulder as it is in the throwing motion, the humerus acts as a lever and tears the biceps tendon and the labrum. The lining of the shoulder joint from the glenoid cavity is torn in a front-to-back fashion, hence the name SLAP—the superior aspect of the labrum is torn from anterior to posterior.

Usually the signs and symptoms involve the player either complaining of pain or instability in the shoulder while throwing. This condition worsens when the player puts his arm into the "cocked position" ready to throw. Some players with this condition may experience pain while doing overhead weight lifting, and some have reported actually hearing a clicking sound in the shoulder when attempting to throw.

Unfortunately this condition is seldom discovered until damage to the labrum has already been done. Athletic trainers and physicians use a clinical test called the shoulder impingement test to identify this condition. The test is performed by stabilizing the rear of the player's shoulder, extending his elbow, and passively forward flexing his arm. If the test is positive for a SLAP lesion, the player will experience pain near the end of the range of motion. Usually an MRI will be done to confirm the diagnosis.

If the damage to the labrum is not significant, withholding the player from activity and prescribing anti-inflammatory medications may treat the condition. Stretching and stabilization exercises, under supervision, can be used when the pain lessens. It is extremely important that the player not return to activity (such as throwing) until the pain has entirely disappeared.

If the labrum is significantly torn, the only viable treatment for someone who wants to continue to be active in the sport is a surgery in which the torn labrum is arthroscopically reattached. After the surgery, it is important that the player undergo supervised rehabilitation designed to strengthen the shoulder muscles and gain flexibility in the joint. Unlike the generally more positive outcomes that result from Tommy John surgery, only a small percentage of players of those who suffer significant labral tears are able to successfully return to anywhere near their previous level of performance. Most often, players who are able to come back lose significant velocity, are forced to alter their mechanics—creating further injury risk—and often retear the labrum. Recent cases such as Mike Sirotka and Mariners prospect Ryan Anderson come to mind as typical. Shawn Green of the Dodgers is a worst-case scenario—Green's labrum was torn too severely to repair, so the damaged cartilage was removed, and he has some bone-on-bone in the shoulder.

Currently available data suggests that the best course of therapy for a torn labrum is to be as conservative as the course of the injury will allow. As it is a very difficult injury to diagnose without visualizing the shoulder (which means either opening it or putting in an arthroscope to look around), it can be a controversial diagnosis and one that a pitcher will often resist.

If possible, a choice between scoping a labrum and an open (classic, scalpel-based) procedure seems to tilt strongly toward the comebacks from players who have had the scope. Players like Robb Nen, Kevin Millwood, and Al Leiter show positive signs of a full return to previous function after having their shoulders scoped.

Further technological developments, such as new labrum surgery automators, stand to make labrum surgery as routine as Tommy John surgery is today. By standardizing and simplifying the surgical procedures of anchoring and securing the labrum through a minimum of invasive points, the odds of recovery stand to improve. Remember, current data points to more success with less invasiveness.

Shoulder injuries have the most rapidly developing rehabilitation protocols due to advances in technology and the number of cases, giving the surgeon the sample size for useful data and therefore good decisions. While a serious shoulder injury is still a near-death experience for a pitching career, less significant shoulder injuries now border on the routine. If we can learn to save each body part, each part of the pitching chain, we will be closer to understanding how to keep any pitcher healthy as a whole.

Elbow

Since the invention of the breaking ball, there has been no more significant development in baseball than Tommy John surgery. The development and continued refinement of the procedure and its coordinated rehab has earned Dr. Frank Jobe a place in the Hall of Fame in the eyes of many. He would be, if so enshrined, the first medical staff to be honored. While I certainly admire many of the writers who are memorialized in that august museum, to argue that any of them had near the impact that Dr. Jobe has had in the space of thirty years is folly.

Due to this advance and other knowledge developed in the broader BMC, elbow injuries tend to respond very well to more aggressive therapies. In the Baseball Prospectus Injury Database, the highest success rate for return from elbow injuries is produced by surgery. Why this should be so is not clear, but it is useful to recall the medhead's rule that shoulder injuries tend to first present as a loss of velocity, while elbow injuries present as a loss of control. A pitcher is more likely to disguise a loss of velocity than to pitch effectively with diminished command.

The most common and best known of the three major elbow injuries is the sprain of the ulnar collateral ligament (UCL). If this is severely torn, a tendon graft can replace the ruined ligament. This operation is now popularly known (and trademarked) as Tommy John surgery, which has been refined from a four-hour experiment to a one-hour patch job. The real work is now being done not on the operating table but in the rehab protocol.

In 2002 Brandon Claussen, a touted lefty in the Yankees organization, found himself on Dr. Jim Andrews's table, an all too familiar place for young pitching prospects. (So many pitching prospects have failed that Joe Sheehan coined a term— TINSTAPP, "There is no such thing as a pitching prospect"—to describe the phenomenon.) Claussen was another data point in Sheehan's TINSTAPP, but more important was that one year after surgery, on a clear June evening, Claussen returned to Yankee Stadium and pitched so effectively that he later was a key component of a major trade.

What was different about what Brandon Claussen and others did from the accepted length of eighteen to twenty-four months for full return to function after gaining the new elbow? While the methods remain a secret, the man who controls the secret is becoming better known, especially within the game.

Mark Littlefield is the head trainer for the New York Yankees' Tampa facility. For years the Yankees have sent their rehabbing players there to enjoy the warm sun and soft grass of its fields. "He's the secret weapon," said a Yankees executive. There are rumors that no fewer than five teams have sought to interview Littlefield, but that the Yankees give him raises in order to keep him in Tampa.

Littlefield is a handsome, athletic guy, looking a bit like he may have been one of the pitchers he now attends to. If the name sounds familiar, yes, he is the younger brother of Pirates general manager Dave Littlefield.

Littlefield and others have honed the rehabilitation of a post–Tommy John elbow to a near science. Here is a typical rehab program for a major league pitcher following Tommy John surgery. It's important to know this information but not to act on it by yourself. If some of the technical or medical terms baffle you, consult your physical therapist.

PHASE ONE, IMMEDIATE MOTION (weeks 0–4)

Goals:

Reestablish nonpainful range of motion (ROM)

Decrease pain and inflammation

Retard muscular atrophy

Protect healing tissue graft site

1. Range of Motion Progression
   a. Posterior splint at 90-degree flexion for 5–7 days
   b. Week 2: functional ROM brace (30–105 degrees); progressive ROM, 5 degrees extension and 10 degrees flexion per week
   c. ROM at least 10–115 degrees in week 3, or full ROM if tolerated
   d. 0–125 degrees in week 4, progress to full flexion; prevent flexion contracture
2. Elbow Joint Compression Dressing (2–3 days)
   a. Wrist and hand ROM and gripping exercises
   b. Ice and compression (assess neurologic status)
   c. Isometrics for shoulder and elbow joint
3. Week 2
   a. Initiate assisted ROM (30–100 degrees)
   b. Continue active assisted ROM
   c. Manual resistance drills (isometrics, tubing)
   d. Scar tissue management
4. Week 3
   a. ROM 15–110 degrees at least
   b. Continue stretching and ROM exercises
   c. Initiate isotonic program; begin with 0 pounds and increase 1 pound each week

    d. Bicycle and easy lower extremity strengthening

    e. Baseline core strengthening

INTERMEDIATE PHASE (weeks 4–7)

    Goals:

    Gradually restore full ROM

    Promote healing of repaired tissue

    Restore strength, power, and endurance

    Restore full function of graft site

1. Week 4

    a. ROM 10–125 degrees at least; assess for flexion contracture and lack of motion

    b. Initiate isotonics for entire arm and shoulder

    c. Active assisted ROM, progressive ROM, stretching

    d. Discontinue brace weeks 4–5

2. Weeks 5–6

    a. Full ROM 0–145 degrees

    b. Continue progression of isotonic strengthening

    c. Manual resistance exercises for elbow and wrist; isotonic strengthening; manual resistance, tubing

    d. Progress core stabilization—incorporate UE movement

    e. Prevent scar tissue maturation

PHASE THREE (weeks 8–13)

    Goals:

    Improve arm strength, power, and endurance

    Maintain full ROM

    Gradually initiate sport activities

1. Weeks 8–10

    a. Thrower's Ten Program

    b. Emphasize following:

        concentric/eccentric biceps

        concentric triceps

stabilization wrist flex/pronaturs
shoulder ER and scapular muscles
  c. Neuromuscular drills
  d. Two-hand plyometrics week 8
     close to body—chest pass and side throw
2. Week 10
  a. Advance two-hand plyometrics away from body
     side-to-side, soccer throws, and side throws
  b. Wrist plyometrics
  c. Continue all exercises
  d. Advanced core program
3. Weeks 12–13
  a. Continue all exercises
  b. May initiate isotonic machine exercises
     bench press
     seated row
     lat pulldowns
     biceps and triceps
  c. Progress to one-hand plyometrics
     90/90 baseball throws

RETURN TO ACTIVITY PHASE (weeks 14–26)
  Goals:
  Continue improvement of power, strength, and endurance
  Gradual return to sports
1. Weeks 14–15
  a. Initiate baseball throws into pitchback
  b. Continue Thrower's Ten Program
  c. Maintain flexibility and stretching
2. Week 16
  a. Initiate interval throwing program (Phase I); full ROM
     and satisfactory stability necessary for return to throwing

3. Weeks 22–26
   a. Initiate interval throwing from mound (Phase II)
   b. Follow with long toss program
4. What to do when the athlete has medial elbow pain when throwing?
   a. Typically flexor-pronator tendonitis rather than UCL
   b. Acute inflammation often from:
      tight wrist flexors
      weak wrist flexors
      decreased shoulder ROM
      weak shoulder ER
   c. Key is to prevent. Do not begin throwing until ready!
   d. Decrease pain and inflammation
      abstain from throwing (1–2 weeks)
      phonophoresis
      iontopatch
      ice
   e. Stretch wrist and shoulder
   f. Continue strengthening

While Littlefield's rehab advances give the Yankees an advantage, secrets seldom stay that way. In sports medicine there is a fine line between altruism and self-interest. While academics seek to publish, trainers seek to heal. Holding new or important knowledge from the broader community only serves the self. While a team may wish to hold an advantage, organizations like the Professional Baseball Athletic Trainers Society (PBATS) do great work making sure not only that their members pass the minimum criteria but that they concentrate on continued education and the dissemination of important information.

Another all too common elbow injury is bone spurs. Spurs are merely small growths of bone—in essence a blister for bone. Bone is not smooth despite its milky white appearance. In the event of irritation or trauma, a bone can defend itself in any number of ways, one of which is often the spur/chip. Chips are nothing more than broken spurs, so there is a direct relationship.

Another elbow injury that is emerging with concerning frequency is damage, including tears, to the flexor tendon in the forearm. The common flexor tendon, attaching at the medial epicondyle, is stressed by the motion of the wrist being pulled forcefully down (flexion). This flexion is part of the pitching motion of a hard sinker or split-finger fastball. The split-fingered grip puts a great deal of stress on the forearm. Combined with the forceful flexion it can, over time or with one "camel's back" pitch, cause the tear.

With most elbow injuries it is difficult to pinpoint the pitch where the injury occurred. Unlike the shoulder, it is possible for a pitcher to throw with a torn ligament or tendon, sometimes effectively. At the end of the 2003 season, Jason Schmidt of the San Francisco Giants pitched the final two months with a torn flexor tendon and showed almost no loss of function. Schmidt is a remarkable talent and was able to remain effective due to an excellent, active medical staff and his ability to function without one of his best pitches, adjusting his output without sacrificing his mechanics.

In the grand scheme, if injury cannot be prevented—and in almost all cases, it can be—an elbow injury can be treated to a stage where the affected pitcher can return to activity. This weak point in the kinetic chain must be watched closely or another great pitcher will lose a year or more of his short pitching career to surgery and rehabilitation.

Hand

The hand and fingers of a pitcher are, of course, necessary for the delivery of the ball. Injuries in this area tend to be minor, with stress transferred to the elbow in most cases where mechanics are in question. Most of the stress placed on the structures of the hand is the result of grips.

As noted in the discussion of the elbow, the split-finger grip carries the most stress among pitches, with the variant forkball closely behind. Most other pitch grips place a minimum of stress and vary little from grip to grip.

Due to the force and texture of the ball leaving the hand, almost always from the tip of the middle finger, some pitchers

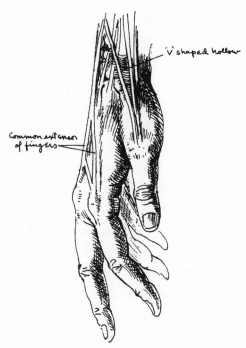

The hand, schematic drawing.

develop skin problems. These problems, usually presenting as cuts or blisters, are not serious in themselves but can reduce short-term effectiveness by preventing a proper grip of the ball. In some cases a chronic skin problem can thwart a pitcher from being in the game long enough to be effective.

Several pitchers in recent years, most notably Jeremy Affeldt of the Kansas City Royals and Josh Beckett of the Florida Marlins, have seen promising careers nearly derailed by blisters. Beckett lost nearly half a season over the last two before finally correcting the problem. Once he was able to pitch without the specter of blisters, Beckett went on to become one of the heroes of the 2003 World Series.

While blisters are a normal response to repetitive friction from pulling against the seams of the ball, the outbreak of blisters among pitchers during 2002 was curious. Most of these pitchers had thrown for years without skin-related problems. What had changed? According to many within the game, there were two possible causes. The most likely is that the texture of the horsehide surface of the ball had been slightly changed. Others said that the stitching of the ball was slightly raised. After speaking with a number of pitchers during the research for this book, I believe it is the latter. Actually, I believe the ball was returned to more normal levels.

In previous seasons the hitters had achieved such an advantage that there were serious discussions about returning the mound to its 1968 height, a season when pitchers had a marked advantage over hitters. While the battle between hitters and pitchers ranges from extreme to extreme and from pole to pole, the lower seams made it more difficult to throw effective breaking pitches.

Pitchers can often be seen tossing a ball back to the umpire if they don't think it has the correct "feel." "Feel? It's the laces

I care about," said one pitcher. "If I get one that's flat [the laces are not sufficiently raised from the surface of the ball], I'm tossing it back. I've gotten a flat one back, thrown a ball away, then got a new one. If I get a good one, I'll keep it in play as long as I can. With the good ones, you can do that. With a bad one, it leaves quickly."

I asked if he felt the balls were different in 2002 and 2003. "They're all different. I couldn't measure it, but I can feel it. I didn't have to toss as many back, so I guess that means something."

Blister "cures" are as varied as they are ineffective. From pickle juice to thrusting the hand into rice, from ointments and salves to urine, few are effective in toughening the skin against the friction. Dodgers trainer Stan Johnston invented one popular cream. Originally designed for bronc riders, Stan's Rodeo Cream is now standard fare in many baseball training rooms. The concoction's recipe is secret and available only by prescription, though many believe that benzene is a major ingredient. Johnston also has a preventive cream that is in wide use.

While Johnston's concoctions have helped, blisters will remain a problem, especially for starters. As long as pitchers throw more than eighty pitches with rough red yarn against their skin, blisters will be a part of baseball. The best way to deal with blisters is simple: when they begin, a player must let his coaches know and, if possible, rest. The earlier a blister is caught, especially at the stage where the skin is just beginning to be irritated—often known as a hot spot—the earlier therapeutic methods can be applied.

While a blister is hardly life threatening or even particularly painful, it is near impossible to pitch effectively with a significant irritation. Also difficult to deal with is a broken or cracked fingernail. Many pitchers will use fake nails to protect one with a small crack. With nails, the only healing program is time, and while prevention is obviously the best treatment, broken nails tend to be traumatic, meaning it is often near impossible to project time lost due to this injury.

Putting It Together

Each of these sections, from the first push to the last touch of horsehide against the finger, concerns a necessary step in pitching. It is a chain of events that somehow allow a man to throw a ball over ninety miles an hour, cause a ball to break and dive away from a batter, and to do it over and over again. The slightest breakdown or weakness in the kinetic chain breaks the ability of the pitcher to perform his activity at full potential.

The ability to put each of these sections in motion in the proper sequence, in a repeatable fashion, leads to the amazing performances we see on major league mounds. The same mechanics work for anyone. With the basics of anatomy in hand, it is these mechanics we must now consider.

5

THE FUNCTIONAL
MECHANICS OF PITCHING

With a knowledge of what parts make up the functional kinetic chain of the ideal pitching motion, we can now look at what events, in sequence, must occur in that motion. It is impossible to describe the ideal pitching motion without discussing the timing in relation to that motion. In this case, a video or seminar is much better as a descriptive or teaching tool than is a book. We'll try to make do. Our advantage is that we can discuss pitching in the abstract, showing what works for every pitcher and avoiding the mistakes our eyes can force upon us.

In order to understand what he was doing in his pitching, Dr. Mike Marshall knew that he couldn't trust his eyes or his pitching coaches. In the late 1960s, Marshall became one of the first pitchers to have his motion filmed by high-speed cameras. He did this during his studies in kinesiology at Michigan State University that led to his doctorate.

"You can argue with me," Marshall says, "but it's harder to argue with Sir Isaac Newton." Marshall has a point. (Newton has been dead since the seventeenth century, making discussion difficult at best.) Instead of basing his teaching on imparted wisdom, each of the parts of Marshall's motion is scientifically based on Newtonian physics.

Immediately, baseball resists such scientific analysis. While there is no shortage of intelligence in the game, trying to find a good discussion of higher math or science will gain a player about as many friends in a locker room as setting fire to someone's cleats. (Well, actually, a good hotfoot can be appreciated in the game.)

I hope you won't have the same reaction to physics. While you certainly don't need a doctorate-level education to make use of it, there are a few simple physical principles to understand before moving on to discuss the application of these laws to pitching.

Newton's First Law deals with inertia: A body remains at rest, or if in motion, it remains in uniform motion with constant speed in a straight line, unless it is acted on by an unbalanced external force. In simpler terms, a ball wants to either stay in the glove or go straight toward the plate. This is a simple experiment. Stand on the mound and put the ball in your glove. Wait. You'll see that the ball indeed does stay in your glove unless you do something with it, like drop it or throw it.

In other words, the ball has no action without the force being imparted to it by the pitcher. But is the second part of this First Law—the straight-line motion—also true? Of course! But a pitcher can intentionally or unintentionally use external forces that cause a ball to move from a straight line, or external forces such as gravity can act on a ball.

The rule of "a straight line is the shortest distance between two points" holds true here as well. While throwing the ball in a straight line is not always the most effective pitch, it is the shortest path to maximize apparent velocity. This straight line will become very important later, so don't let go of the concept.

We move on to Newton's Second Law, which deals with acceleration, a topic near and dear to every pitcher's heart. This law says: The acceleration produced by an unbalanced force acting on an object is proportional to the magnitude of the net force, in the same direction as the force, and inversely proportional to the mass of the object.

It is difficult to simplify this law. In essence it gives us the groundwork for determining how much force is necessary to create the acceleration that is desired. Through algebraic calculations, Marshall is able to identify the forces necessary to accelerate a ball from rest to the maximum possible velocity.

Using this calculation and observed pitching motions, Marshall first determined that most pitchers in the major leagues threw a fastball that traveled at ninety miles per hour. He also was able to determine through a study of high-speed film that the average time of force application was two-tenths of a second. Using these as parts of the calculation, Marshall determined that a pitcher must exert just over six and a half pounds of pressure on the ball for two-tenths of a second in order to create the desired ninety-mile-an-hour fastball. (Marshall actually uses feet per second in his calculations—132 feet per second sounds a lot more impressive.)

Within the bounds of this Second Law and the calculations, it is easy to see how to increase the velocity of a pitch. The pitcher must either increase the force applied to the ball or increase the length of time the force is applied. Subtracting 25 percent, of application time forces a pitcher to increase the applied force by 33 percent. Increasing the application time by only 10 percent, to 0.22 seconds, increases the velocity of the pitch over eight miles per hour, to ninety-eight miles per hour. Yes, it's that simple—in the calculations if not the application—to gain velocity.

The Third Law brought to us by Sir Isaac Newton is perhaps the most widely known: For every Action force, there is an equal and oppositely directed Reaction force.

Given the rules and practicalities of baseball, there are only a few choices for the pitcher in generating these forces. He can push against the rubber, against the ground, or even against himself.

One school of pitching instruction, widely advertised, has as its most basic teaching this gem: "Do not push off." Instead, pitching coaches who subscribe to this theory teach their pitchers to merely "fall" off the mound from the ready position. The law of reaction shows that while it is certainly possible to generate force from another location, the First and Second Laws suggest that the easiest way would be to drive off the available anchor in a straight line toward home plate. If someone does not wish to use all the available tools, they may be successful, but they will certainly require more work.

Newton's knowledge in hand, we can now apply his principles toward an ideal pitching motion. While it is unlikely that any pitcher at any level can have ideal form on every pitch, by being close to it, or at least avoiding the most damaging flaws, a pitcher can avoid the most dangerous of technique injuries. Just the term "technique injuries" is a very powerful concept. Using the proper techniques even within expanded parameters of what is considered prudent usage, injury can be minimized or even completely avoided.

The ideal form for pitching is something of a Platonic ideal. It will seldom be truly perfect in the real world, and we must remember Law's Rule (named for sabermetrician Keith Law of the Toronto Blue Jays): sometimes tinkering with an effective motion can make a pitcher less effective, even if more efficient. The key to finding the ideal form for an individual pitcher is not to mold every pitcher into a one-size-fits-all motion, but to bring each pitcher closer to the ideal within the bounds of his own effectiveness.

From the ready position in either the stretch or the windup, the ideal motion brings the shoulders in a direct line with the elbows. In this position, called "Flex T" by Tom House, the pitcher should be able to have a broomstick held from elbow point to elbow point. The pitching elbow must never go behind this theoretical line. Doing so would cause the arm to pull across the body and add force that could cause the forearm to fly open and put unneeded and damaging force on the inside of the elbow.

The theoretical line of the shoulders does not need to cross another theoretical line from home plate to second base. Instead the shoulder line should not rotate beyond pointing the pitching shoulder (right or left, as appropriate) directly at second base. Additional rotation at this point exposes the ball and requires that the pitcher bring the ball back in an arc to come to the driveline.

The driveline, you will remember, is yet another theoretical line from the ball in the Flex T position, past the pitcher's ball-side ear, and straight to the catcher's mitt. Of course, with breaking balls, the path of the ball will alter from the driveline due to external forces. The driveline may be theoretical in nature, but it is absolute as well.

The pitching foot (same side of the body as the pitching hand, or "ball-side") should be turned slightly forward of parallel to the pitching rubber. The angle can be adjusted to comfort, but the pitcher and coach should seek to find the angle where the front of the thigh and glutes are doing more of the work than the inner or outer thigh. It is no secret that the thigh is stronger in front than inside. Do you know anyone who can kick a ball farther using an abduction motion? Yet this is exactly what most pitchers are taught to do! The proper motion for maximal force generation is more akin to the "donkey kick" motion than to a jumping jack.

It is not important for the pitcher to raise his leg a significant height, but it is important for the pitcher to maintain a balanced, strong position. While some pitchers, such as Nolan Ryan or Dontrelle Willis, can use a high leg kick to recruit additional force, most pitchers will only throw off their balance and waste force and momentum out of the driveline. I would recommend that a pitcher raise his leg as high as he is comfortable and balanced, but my bias is to keep the leg even with or lower than the "thigh flat at waist level" used by most pitchers.

Pushing uniformly, not suddenly, off the rubber, the hips begin to turn, generating velocity. The shoulder line turns not just from a home-second to first-third orientation, but instead goes powerfully through a 180-degree turn, moving from home-second to second-home. The stride leg is moving forward, carrying both the center of gravity and the driveline release point forward.

As the center of gravity moves over the front foot, the front leg does not act as a block. Instead the pitcher continues to "walk" forward over the front leg in a straight line parallel or equivalent to the driveline. There is actual force production by the glove-side foot as the pitcher continues his motion forward. As the shoulder line reaches its point of maximum velocity, the forearm powerfully accelerates from its cocked position near the upper arm, adding to the force applied to the ball. This late movement of the forearm not only generates velocity but does so at a location that will cause the release point of the ball to be slightly ahead of that by pitchers using a traditional motion—sometimes by as much as one foot. Shortening the distance the ball travels creates an apparent increase in velocity and reduces the batter's reaction time.

It is important to note that this actual reduction in distance and apparent increase in velocity is the one true advantage that a taller pitcher has over a shorter pitcher. While Randy Johnson (standing six feet eleven inches) throws his fastball at ninety-five miles per hour, Billy Wagner (standing five feet eleven inches on his tiptoes) can also generate that velocity and more. But a study of their motions in game film shows that Johnson releases the ball nearly eighteen inches closer to the plate. This small reduction in distance gives Johnson's ball an apparent four-mile-per-hour "boost." It is, in effect, as if Johnson were pitching from a different mound, one built at fifty-nine feet from home plate rather than the regulation sixty feet, six inches.

As the forearm accelerates, it also powerfully pronates. Pronation in this sense is the motion that turns the thumb of the pitching hand down or re-creates the motion of pouring out a glass. This pronation motion not only gives a final boost of acceleration to the ball but protects the elbow, allowing a natural deceleration.

The ball is released in varying fashions according to the intention of the pitcher, but in all instances the last point of contact will be the tip of the middle finger. Even with a curveball that will often apparently last contact the index finger, high-speed video shows that the ball rolls over the index finger with the middle fingertip imparting the last contact and force.

As the ball is released, the pitcher continues forward rather than overrotating and falling off to either side of the driveline. Not only will this put the pitcher in a good defensive position, it will ensure that a maximum of force is directed in the driveline and imparted to the ball.

An illustration of pronation of the forearm, as
Mark Prior throws.

The ideal motion uses a longer force application to increase
the velocity of the ball, reduces unnecessary and counterproductive motion, and directs all forces over the driveline to increase both control and apparent velocity, all while reducing the
need for the body—specifically the elbow and shoulder—to ac-
cept and dissipate energy. Just as the creation of light creates
heat as waste, pitching can never completely apply all force to
the ball. Wasted energy must go somewhere—another physical

law, this time in thermodynamics—and in pitching, most of the energy is either misdirected or brought inward to generate force on parts of the body.

As a pitcher nears the ideal motion, he will begin to feel it as a fluid process, the ball becoming a lightning bolt or beam of light directed in a straight line from hand to catcher's mitt. No matter the pitch—fastball, breaking ball, or change-up—this motion and energy is nearly the same: bringing the ball through the driveline, using the kinetic chain and Newtonian physics to throw the ball past the batter for strikes.

Some of you probably paused over the words "breaking ball" and "change-up." In relation to the ideal motion, the changes that a pitcher makes to throw other than a fastball are extremely minor and external to the force application through the driveline. A breaking ball uses spin and fluid dynamics to impart external forces that move the ball off the driveline after release, while a change-up exploits a mechanical inefficiency to deceive the batter and change his timing. A knuckleball is a wholly different beast but requires an even greater attention to mechanics to be effective.

While I might talk about the methods of throwing the various pitches—the two- or four-seam fastball, the cutter, the curve, the hammer, the screwball, the knuckler, the circle change, the slider, the palmball, the forkball, the splitter, or any of the twenty-eight legal variations that I know of—there are better ways to learn these pitches and better people to learn them from. Performed properly, no pitch is more damaging than any other. The concept of "pitch cost"—that a breaking ball inflicts more damage than a fastball—is true only in cases where a pitcher performs either pitch with significant mechanical inefficiencies.

But I should add that I do not believe in "curveballs" or "sliders"; to me they are all "breaking balls." Simply put, there

Prior's Grips

Fastball, top view.

Fastball, side view.

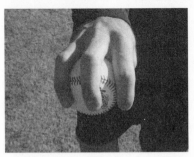

Change-up, top view.

Change-up, side view.

Breaking ball, three-quarter view.

Breaking ball, side view.

are several pitches that seek to use outside forces to move the ball off the driveline and increase the motion and deception that a batter must deal with while attempting to put the ball in play. An ideal curveball breaks "12 to 6" or "falls off the table." The reason the ball performs this way is that the pitcher, by use of grip and release, causes the ball to rotate in a certain manner. The seams and ball surface interact with the air during the flight of the ball; following scientific laws as inflexible as Bernoulli's Principle and the Magnus Effect, these forces cause a ball to move.

Only the difference in rotation distinguishes one variety of breaking ball from another. A "12 to 6" curveball can easily be adjusted by turning the position of the hand slightly, becoming a "2 to 8" slider. A screwball, one of the most difficult pitches to master, is merely a reverse curveball. While the mechanics of the screwball are different—releasing the ball during and not before pronation—the actions on the ball are the same.

Any motion caused by the intentional rotation of the ball is so similar that it can be accurately described as a breaking ball. A pitcher who understands the principles behind the breaking ball should be able to adjust his delivery in order to make the ball act like any of these pitches. While differentiation may help in the description of these pitches, it does nothing toward easing the teaching of them. To me and to science, a breaking ball is a breaking ball. As Shakespeare might have said, "A breaking ball by any other name is still decelerated by gravity at a rate of thirty-two feet per second." Come to think of it, he probably wouldn't have said that.

A pitcher in possession of good mechanics is near priceless. This pitcher will throw effectively, has a base in which to control a variety of pitch variations, will have less injury and soreness, can pitch deeper into games, and will increase his velocity, both real and apparent. That pitcher is going to be one batters do not want to face.

6

ASSESSING MECHANICS

If you follow baseball—and if you're reading this I assume you have more than a passing interest—you've heard discussions about pitchers having good or bad mechanics. Few observers, however, have the skills to break down the kinetic chain of events in order to accurately point out weak points or correctable situations. Many pitching coaches working in the game have weaknesses in assessing mechanics. Some coaches will even argue that high-speed film or computer analysis of the pitcher's motion is necessary because some flaws are visible only at speeds well below what we see in game.

Just as there are absolute laws and relative functions, some flaws are offshoots of physical realities. Each of these flaws is correctable. By definition, if there is a perfect, ideal motion, each flaw is in no way permanent or uncorrectable. But coaching can become difficult when a flawed pitcher gains an advantage, in perceived comfort, deception, or what I call "bad velocity."

Bad velocity is the idea that some pitchers can throw with greater velocity using poor, even damaging mechanics, than they can initially using proper mechanics. This is a function, of course, of neuromuscular memory and training. Over time a pitcher committed to proper mechanics will usually find more velocity once the motion becomes more natural. There are exceptions as well as practical concerns. As Law's Rule states, sometimes tinkering is counterproductive.

There is a value decision to be made when a pitcher is flawed yet successful. Pitchers such as Kyle Peterson, Nick Neugebauer, and Craig House (no relation to Tom House) have made it to the major leagues using mechanics that are at best flawed and at worst freakish. (In some of the more colorful baseball writing in recent memory, Peterson's delivery was described thus: "It appears that, for just a second in the middle of his delivery, he is a puppet with his strings cut, going limp and dropping, then suddenly coming back to life." House, on the other hand, was described as "all knees and elbows, leaping off the rubber with his head exploding upward like a Rock 'Em–Sock 'Em Robot game.") A pitching coach, team, or organization must look themselves in the mirror to decide whether they will allow a pitcher to continue with damaging mechanics, hoping to ride that success for a short time, or commit to helping the pitcher change. Too many organizations and coaches take the easy way out.

Changing mechanics, especially those that have been ingrained into muscles over years of competition, is difficult and requires an intense commitment. Doing so inside of a season or even in a pre-season does not likely provide enough time to do so properly. In Florida, Dr. Marshall conducts a nine-month pitching program that will, he says, make a pitcher injury-proof. What can be done is to correct individual, discrete flaws that will bring a pitcher closer to ideal within his personal effectiveness. The more flaws or the more profound, the harder the mechanics will be to correct—but those are precisely the pitchers who need help most. Taking a pitcher with two major flaws down to one certainly has benefits.

Almost all flaws can be classified as errors of efficiency; attempting to break Newtonian laws doesn't pay. Whether fighting inertia or reducing distances of force application, correcting or reducing these flaws is imperative for any pitcher who wants long-term success. Some flaws are more apparent than others, but let's take a brief look at some of the most damaging and most common mistakes.

The single most damaging and common flaw is inwardly rotating the upper arm. As I explained previously, moving off the driveline forces the body to use muscles to decelerate the arm rather than have the motion naturally terminate. The stress is focused on the supraspinatus muscle, one of the four rotator cuff muscles. When this is done over and over again, the result is often an impingement. Impingement syndrome is where the humeral head closes the anatomical gap between it and the acromion process. In a proper motion, the humerus does not inwardly rotate, minimizing this impingement. Any time you hear "impingement" or "tendonitis in the shoulder," the likely culprit is a mechanical inefficiency in the upper arm.

Another extremely common flaw is pulling the arm across the body. Besides taking energy away from the driveline and requiring additional geometric complexity, it also stresses the teres minor, another of the four muscles that makes up the rotator cuff. It is imperative that the pitcher lock the shoulders into a strong "Flex T" position to prevent this adverse process. The strong Flex T is so important that it must be taught early and emphasized often. Any pitching coach who allows one of his players to weaken this position is not a real pitching coach; he is an advance scout for orthopedic surgeons.

One of the more common flaws among advanced pitchers is what Dr. Marshall calls "forearm flyout." When a pitcher takes his elbow/forearm beyond the line of the Flex T, he is creating a situation where the ulnar collateral ligament is in danger. By overrotating the upper arm, the centripetal force will not only push the ball out of the driveline but will cause the bones of the elbow to slam together. While a physical collision is not often apparent or even traumatic, the continual collisions reduce the flexion potential of the elbow, putting stress on the ligaments. With repeated stress on the ligament, the ligament itself begins to break down. While Tommy John surgery is near miraculous, it is performed too often because this flaw is not corrected.

Forearm flyout is not only a problem of mechanics, it is the product of fatigue. As a pitcher tires, he often will need to "reach back" to find or maintain velocity. This reaching back is often quite literal, overrotating the arm and creating force that is counterproductive in order to maintain the level the pitcher perceives as necessary. Perfect mechanics and adequate conditioning are important to render this type of behavior unnecessary.

Slightly different than forearm flyout, but with much the same result, is an interrelated flaw of hand position. It feels natural for many pitchers to point the ball toward second base. This rotation of the wrist is not only unnecessary, it exposes the ball to the batter. Combined with an overrotation, this gives the batter nearly an additional half-second and at least six additional reference points for seeing and recognizing the pitch. Obviously the pitcher who "palms out" with the ball is not only hurting himself, he is hurting his chances to get the batter out.

Another common flaw that stresses the ulnar collateral is keeping the forearm near a vertical position as the body rotates. In addition to reducing the force that can be imparted as the forearm accelerates by shortening the distance and, in essence, breaking the important kinetic chain, the stresses placed on the elbow during rotation in this position can cause ligament damage. The shoulder is also unnecessarily recruited into the process, reducing both the efficiency and power of the motion.

Footwork is very important to the kinetic chain, and two flaws involving the feet are common. If the front foot lands in a closed position (toes pointing to the ball side) rather than pointing directly to the plate, the pitcher is forced to throw across his body and force is moved out of the driveline. It does the pitcher no good to apply force in any direction other than through the driveline. Since there is a finite amount of force that can be applied to the baseball, any inefficiency will be immediately noted as a loss of velocity.

Dealing with the pitching rubber also causes flaws and inefficiencies. As detailed, the force for the pitching motion must start in the feet as the pitcher pushes off the ground and moves toward home plate. Techniques such as "drop and drive" or sudden strong pushes off the pitching rubber are counterproductive, accelerating the center of gravity beyond what can be controlled by most pitchers. The ideal motion is a steady push off the rubber, followed by a "walking" motion by the ball-side leg. It is also important that the force off the rubber is made parallel—actually, in line with the driveline. The stride must be as long as possible, usually a distance close to the pitcher's height but not too long, which would drop the center of gravity and put unneeded stress on the glove-side knee. The stride also must allow for continued force production by pushing off the glove-side leg during the pitching motion.

A simple test can determine if the stride is too long. Simulate the pitching motion to the point where the glove-side foot contacts the ground. As this contact is made, the pitcher should attempt to jump straight up in the air, using only the force of the glove-side leg. If the pitcher has overextended his stride, he will have a difficult time generating enough force to counteract his forward momentum.

The final common flaw is one that somehow remains controversial, despite extensive research. In an ideal motion, as the ball is released, the pitcher should powerfully pronate the forearm. Pronation, you will remember, is the action of rotating the thumb downward. For a right-handed pitcher, this will be a counterclockwise rotation from roughly nine o'clock to six o'clock. Failing to pronate the arm will not only reduce the force generated as the ball is delivered, but it puts the elbow at risk.

The proper motion for a breaking ball is very similar to that of using a hammer. (Either grab a hammer or simulate the action as you read this.) As the hammer is brought down toward the nail by the action of extending the arm, there is a point where either the hammer will impact the nail or the arm will fully extend and "lock."

By removing the impact, we illustrate the problem of throwing a breaking ball improperly. Grasping the hammer, imagine there is a nail at about waist height. As you gently bring the hammer down—do *not* do this full force—the absence of impact slowing the hammer is transferred to the arm and in most cases, the elbow takes the brunt, locking out and threatening to hyperextend.

The same occurs with a breaking ball, unless a pitcher pronates his arm. Leo Mazzone, the pitching coach of the Atlanta Braves, in his book *Pitch Like a Pro*, advocates pulling the elbow in to the body to cushion, but let's try this, again using the hammer. As the hammer comes to the theoretical waist-level nail, just before the elbow extends fully, turn the elbow inward, as if you were trying to touch your elbow to your waist. You'll

feel the humeral head turn sharply in the glenoid fossa as it re-
verses direction suddenly. The shoulder itself is forced forward
and, depending on how much downward rotational force is in
play, the elbow may extend fully anyway if the biceps is unable
to slow the extension. In most arms the triceps is much stronger
than the biceps—most people can lift more in a bench press
than they can curl.

Now, again with the hammer, let's aim for the theoretical
nail, but just before the elbow locks out, pronate the arm. Remember, pronation means that you will rotate the wrist inward,
turning the head of the hammer toward the floor. Instead of hyperextending the elbow, the force is now used to complete the
follow through, and deceleration falls to the skeleton rather
than the muscles, tendons, and ligaments.

Pronation at the end of every pitch is not unnatural. In fact
it is purely natural, using the strongest component to do the
most work and not ignoring inertia. Simply but powerfully put,
*using any pitching motion that does not end in pronation will
likely eventually end in injury*. High-speed photography as well
as anecdotal evidence has proven that all pitchers at any level
tend to end in pronation. Why fight it?

While the flaws and mechanical efficiencies discussed here
are certainly not an exhaustive list, they are the most common
and most damaging. By eliminating these flaws in a pitcher, the
reduction in the risk and number of injuries would be astound-
ing. While any pitching coach or parent can help with the correction of mechanics, pitching is like having an injury: at some
point you want to consult with the best. In books, videos, and
clinics, the best pitching coaches in the world are available. I
highly recommend using these and any other available resources for improving and protecting—and ultimately saving—
our pitchers.

7

CORRECTING MECHANICS

Professional pitching coaches are well paid—perhaps not what they are worth, but certainly well, either by teams or by the pitcher or his parents. In return for this consideration, every pitching coach should know not only how to get the most from his charges, but what techniques will get them to the point where they can be successful.

Hall of Fame basketball coach Bob Knight says, "The duty of a coach is to give his players a chance to win." A pitching coach must be able to do everything necessary to give his pitcher the chance to win—or he must know enough to send his charge to an expert. I don't expect every pitching coach to be an expert on diet, rehabilitation, or biomechanics, but I do expect each pitching coach to seek out the state of the art in these fields and to have access to the work of the experts in each field. While every coach cannot be Tom House, every coach can have Tom's books and videos. In each field necessary for the multi-disciplinary approach to successful pitching, a coach himself must have mentors.

When it comes to teaching the science of pitching, it is almost as necessary to unteach years of poor mechanics and ingrained inefficiencies as it is to drill until the proper methods are natural actions. It is important for pitching coaches to know the keys to delivery and to recognize the points and flaws in order to properly instruct his charges. Whether it is a professional coach, a volunteer, or a parent, by allowing your player or your son to take the mound, you are also taking responsibility for the consequences he faces.

Many pitchers who read this book will become one of the most difficult things to be in all of sports—their own coach. Through modern technologies such as video cameras, it is possible for athletes themselves to note their own flaws and inefficiencies. In some cases athletes are their own coach because the one provided for them does not meet the standards of the profession, failing to meet the definitions of a true coach. Worse, a pitcher may deal with a coach who teaches counterproductive methods or insists that his wrongheaded, old-school, my-way-or-the-highway teachings, passed down to him from another guy who didn't really know what he was doing, are the only way to success. Faced with that dilemma, I'd often suggest "the highway" to be the best alternative.

In my work as an injury analyst, I often discuss pitching mechanics in relation to both injury risk and injury cause. Many people ask what I look for and how I determine that mechanics are "good" or "bad." It is important to remember that, within the bounds of Law's Rule, there *is* an absolute, an ideal pitching delivery. Being able to focus on certain keys helps one to do basic analysis of motions, whether for deciding what to work on in the next practice or for predicting the next patient headed for surgery.

The first key is the Flex T position. Pitchers who do not bring the elbows and upper arms into line with the shoulders, both horizontally and vertically, are asking for problems. Pitchers with low or high arms will be mechanically inefficient.

The Flex T position.

Moreover, taking the arms beyond the straight line that goes from elbow to shoulder to shoulder to elbow is asking for tendonitis. A correction for this problem is drills to lock the arms in line. Taping a stick or broom handle across the back of the shoulders can be a great illustrative tool.

You'll notice that "arm slot" is never mentioned. Arm slot is defined as the angle of the forearm in relation to the upper arm. The best research indicates that there is no ideal arm slot. As long as the upper arm remains level with the plane of the shoulders, throwing "over the top," three-quarters, or even sidearm is acceptable.

The second key also occurs in the Flex T position, but this time is focused on the forearm of the pitching side. The forearm should be flexed, brought close to the upper arm in order to powerfully extend. If the forearm is vertical or even extended, there will be serious mechanical inefficiencies and unneeded stress on the ulnar collateral ligament. Keeping the arm flexed could well be named the "Tommy John Prevention Position." A correction for this is repetitive drilling to create muscle memory. An exaggeration drill, in which the ball must touch the shoulder before going into the motion, could be helpful.

The next key is overrotation. If a pitcher's elbow points to the fielder on either side of second base (second baseman for right-handers, shortstop for southpaws), the pitcher is overrotating. This creates unnecessary centripetal force and can cause both shoulder and elbow problems. A correction for this is to emphasize the need for hip acceleration with drills to help the pitcher generate velocity. Another correction is to use an upright but not solid device to "tap" the pitcher when he goes beyond the theoretical line between home and second. I suggest using a broom handle placed in a hitting tee.

The next key is what Tom House calls "stacked and stable." Throughout the motion the pitcher should keep his eyes (and by proxy his head) upright and in line. This will force the spine to remain upright, in a stable position from hips to head. On a mound there will be slight extension of the stride in order to compensate for the downhill motion, the head should move in a line parallel to the ball driveline, and the pitcher's release point will move slightly toward home plate.

Roger Clemens nearly fails this test. During his motion, as he begins to drive forward from his balanced leg raise, Clemens slightly "tick-tocks" his head. He is strong enough to bring it forward fast enough to catch up with his motion and not disrupt a significant amount of energy flow. But this motion is inefficient and forces some of the energy that could be in the driveline to a downward plane, forcing Clemens to raise his back leg more quickly than would be ideal.

Clemens's back leg brings us to the next key, the back foot drag. In an ideal motion, the energy is moving completely forward, along the driveline and in perfect balance. If the torso causes energy to move from the forward driveline to a path below this, the back leg will be forced to come up as a counterweight. This counterweight does bring a dynamic balance, but it also moves slightly backward in relation to the driveline and rotates with the torso in a clockwise fashion, as seen from the third-base side.

Both of these flaws—the unstable spine and the raised back leg—tend to be caused by a weak core. A greater focus on strength and plyometric training of the abdominals, obliques, and other key muscles of the core is necessary. This core training should be a major part of any pitcher's fitness program. Most pitchers, even professionals, have severe strength and endurance deficits in their core, robbing them of a key ingredient in their delivery. In the kinetic chain, all parts must be strong. Imagine placing two metal plates on the top and bottom of a block of Jell-O. No matter how strong and solid the plates are, the Jell-O will not allow for much transfer of energy between them. A weak core is too often the pitcher's Jell-O. The strongest legs or fastest arm will be wasted or, worse, overstressed in attempts to compensate for the weak core.

The final key is hip rotation. As I have said innumerable times thus far and surely more before you reach the back cover, there is a near one-to-one relationship between hip and pitch velocity. Dr. Glenn Fleisig of the American Sports Medicine

Institute has most notably documented this phenomenon in numerous studies. It is difficult to watch a pitcher and not be distracted by the motion of his arm, but if you can focus on his hips, you can learn much more about the pitcher than you can by looking at his hands. If the pitcher's hips lag or appear slow, you can be sure that the pitch will be much the same. The correction for slow hips is drills that focus on hip rotation and velocity, such as "tap" drills where an object is placed 180 degrees from the original hip position and is "tapped" by the hip itself. It is important that this be an object that is not solid! On his own, any pitcher can simply simulate this motion, concentrating on proper mechanics and hip velocity.

In a later chapter we'll focus more on drills, but suffice it to say that there are other books, videos, and teaching devices to go to for help. Correcting mechanical flaws and inefficiencies is perhaps the most important job of the pitching coach, but it is certainly not the only one. While it is the coach's job to keep his pitchers' tools sharp and ready, he should also keep his own tools state of the art. The minute a coach stops learning, his job and his players are at risk.

Double-spin Mechanics—the Future?

The science of pitching always seems to be about two steps behind actual practice. The work Tom House did a decade ago is now becoming general knowledge because of the success of his students like Robb Nen, Randy Johnson, and Mark Prior. Each year the media wonders if Leo Mazzone's principles will work—again. For Rick Peterson and Dr. Mike Marshall, their academic bent is to avoid the mainstream, but people inside the game are finally beginning to take notice of their results.

While work in the United States concentrates on spreading a basic understanding of scientific principles, new advances in Japan will likely have an impact on baseball for years to come. Called "New Motion Principles," "Gyromechanics," and "Synchronized Spin Mechanics" in some places, mostly due to the vagaries of translation from Japanese to English, I will call this "double-spin mechanics" (DSM) for both simplicity and the descriptive nature of the term.

The most basic tenet of DSM is that pitchers must coordinate two separate spinning motions in order to make pitches accurately and effectively. The first spin is that of the torso and is no different from the hip turn that generates force in the ideal Newtonian model. The second spin is the rotation of the arm as it moves through its motion. This is different from the Newtonian model in that DSM attempts to generate force from the humeral rotation rather than from arm extension. Both, however, end with powerful pronation of the forearm.

In two ways the training methods and results of DSM differ significantly from the work of Americans. First, DSM requires a great deal of synchronization and focuses on timing over the kinetic chain. Second, done properly, DSM allows for something new to come from the motion—a new pitch.

Daisuke Matsuzaka is best known as one of Japan's Olympic heroes from his days as a schoolboy, taking Japan's baseball team to the 2000 medal round. While the Americans came away with the gold, the Japanese had their eighteen-year-old hero. Matsuzaka went from high school to the Japanese pros, almost immediately becoming the ace of the Seibu Lions. He did so on the basis of two pitches: a mid-nineties fastball and a "gyroball."

Yes, a gyroball. The pitch is seldom seen in America, but Matsuzaka's devastating pitch has been watched on video and by scouts who hope that Matsuzaka becomes the next Ichiro or Hideo Nomo in the American major leagues. The gyroball is the purest result of DSM, coming out of the hand with a hard planar spin. From the batter's perspective, a gyroball will have a counterclockwise spin around an axis parallel to the ground.

Like a breaking ball, the gyroball follows a curvilinear path from the pitcher's hand to its endpoint, presumably in the catcher's mitt. Unlike a normal breaking ball, the gyroball makes a much harder "left turn," moving away from a right-handed batter. There is not a great deal of vertical movement, but the sharp planar break makes it extremely difficult to get the bat head on the ball squarely, so contact tends to result in a weak grounder to the opposite field.

Critics of the gyroball note that Matsuzaka has developed elbow problems. But it is very difficult to pin his problems on the pitch. Matsuzaka has been used very heavily at a young age, clearing two hundred innings twice before the age of twenty-three. It will require more than one data point to determine the efficacy of DSM. Luckily, it is making inroads against entrenched old-school Japanese baseball thought.

Unlike American baseball, the Japanese game has not adopted much in the way of pitch-count control. In fact Japanese baseball is much closer in usage patterns to American collegiate baseball, where pitch counts can often reach 150 and usage patterns can be odd due to the varying schedule of play. Japanese coaches will also force pitchers to throw additional pitches in the bullpen after unsuccessful starts.

Predictably, Japanese pitchers anecdotally have a higher incidence of overuse injuries but, oddly, a lower incidence of surgery. Due to the paucity of available translated data, it is impossible at this point to pinpoint a cause. Some suggestions have included cultural differences in outlook, valuing the team over the individual. The supposition is that Japanese teams do not consider rehabilitation as fitting their "warrior" or corporate culture. With the value placed on the best players, I doubt this is true, but again, we're just guessing.

DSM is a viable model for training pitchers. Perhaps its best chance for making inroads into American baseball is the importation and success of one of its best products. Matsuzaka is still years away from his free agency, so by that point we'll likely see more students of the method pitching in the Japanese leagues. A team looking for an advantage would do well by looking to be the first to bring a DSM pitcher to America, at any level.

8

CONDITIONING THE PITCHER

Sport Specificity

The best way to get ready to pitch is to pitch.

Wow, profound. Almost zen. Yet this seemingly simple principle is often overlooked. The same holds true for any activity and is known as "specificity." While someone could train for a marathon by swimming, it's not a popular method. Why? After all, someone could build cardiovascular endurance by either method. The principle of specificity helps guide us.

Athletes in various sports often have very different body types. While there is some selection to this principle—tall skinny people play basketball, tall fat guys play offensive line—it is also specificity that produces the specific body type associated with each sport. A mere physical inspection of Lance Armstrong's powerful thighs or expanded lung capacity would lead many to think he was a bicyclist. The long muscles and small stature of someone like Michelle Kwan would lead most to guess that she was a figure skater or perhaps a gymnast.

There is not one body type for pitchers. If we could make a police lineup of Randy Johnson, Greg Maddux, David Wells, and Billy Wagner, few if any people who did not follow baseball closely would recognize them as pitchers. Indeed, most of them do not even appear to fit into the popular mental image of "athlete." Forget chiseled muscles and popping veins when it comes to these world-class athletes. This is not a modern phenomenon either—pitchers have always had varied body types and deliveries, even to the point where there's a guy with three fingers in the Hall of Fame, largely because of what having just three fingers did to his pitches.

Pitchers do not have one specific body type because their success is the result of mechanical efficiency. Each of these athletes—indeed, any successful pitcher of any appearance—can perform certain athletic skills in a very specific manner, none of which result in an outward body change. Aside from pitching, there is almost no other physical activity that does not cause a profound outward body change. Some have argued that pitching is not an unnatural act; in fact, this lack of change has been argued to be the result of pitching, or at the very least throwing, being one of the more natural acts there is. In his book *The Throwing Madonna*, William H. Calvin of the University of Washington argues that the act of hunting with thrown stones helped develop the brain and prepared it for language. While this is quite a leap, it does help explain why throwing is so natural for many. Calvin even calls muscle sequencing the "fastball effect."

Pitchers are successful because they pitch well. Again, this seems about two steps beyond simplistic—and it is. Just as a good teacher wouldn't ask you to learn Spanish by listening to French, it makes as much sense for a coach to ask you to learn to pitch by doing anything other than pitching. Yes, there are times that simulating an activity can approach the effectiveness of the activity itself, but this efficiency is never 100 percent.

Some coaches have a similar bias toward breaking down activities into their component parts. In early stages when a coach

Mark Prior and Tom House observing a young
pitcher.

is seeking to instill proper habits in those who do not yet have
bad habits, or in a situation where a pitcher's mechanics are so
problematic that using them may cause physical damage, simulated or broken-down activities make sense. One common example is "mirror pitching." In this drill a pitcher simply stands
in front of a mirror as he goes through his motion. But I have
yet to see a pitcher in a mirror pitching session use a head
placement identical to the one he uses on a mound. Also,
watching a pitching motion head-on is not the easiest angle
from which to detect mechanical inefficiencies (and yes, this
also holds true for catchers).

Earlier I spoke of a small change that Stan Conte, head trainer for the San Francisco Giants, made to his team's training regimen. By running their windsprints with a ninety-degree curve, they simulated the activity they actually wished to get better at—running the bases. This small, logical change reduced the team's incidence of hamstring injuries dramatically. For pitchers, I have never seen the value in windsprints. I would much rather see pitchers run bases or, better, do a series of sprints from the mound to first, such as they will have to make when covering the bag on a grounder to the first baseman. By adding in a toss to the end of the sprint, the activity not only becomes conditioning, it becomes practice for one of the pitcher's more important defensive plays.

Another activity that is common in pitching workouts is the use of weighted balls. Often made of iron or a similar metal, these balls are intended to increase the work of the arm. They do this, but is the gain worth the risk? That question remains unanswered at the moment because there is no scientific evidence on either side, but common sense tells us that the exercise is of dubious value for most pitchers. In order to keep the pitcher's mechanics identical during a workout, the weighted ball cannot be significantly heavier than a normal ball. Any change to pitching mechanics in practice makes it less likely that the pitcher will learn his proper, repeatable motion. For some pitchers, weighted balls may help, but to coaches I would offer one small piece of advice: if you choose to use this tool, watch your pitchers closely. If there is a mechanical change, take the weighted ball out of that pitcher's hand.

Research by Dr. Frank Jobe has shown that the stress created by pitching is transferred from the muscles and bones to the ligaments at or near 75 percent, based on maximal effort. Within reason, a pitcher should be able to throw any number of pitches below this threshold safely. In other words, as long as your pitcher is throwing at 75 percent effort or less, the best drill is throwing. Drills from the Atlanta Braves' Leo Mazzone concentrate on throwing at these submaximal levels for control and what he calls "feel." This principle tells us why warm-up pitches are not counted in normal pitch counts.

Understanding the principle of sport specificity is important for any athlete or coach in any sport. Pitching is perhaps the most specific motion, one where there is no efficient simulation. In designing or using any drill, it is important to keep principles of specificity in mind. If you cannot adequately answer the question, "How does this directly translate to a specific game action?" the drill should at least be rethought, often scrapped altogether.

As a coach of fourteen- and fifteen-year-olds, I had one practice technique: we played games. While there were often adjustments due to lack of two complete teams (such as "any ball hit to the right/left side of second is an out"), the technique of using game action and simulation to prepare a team works. Using pitchers in a low-stress environment, where they can strengthen their arms and work on technique, and where the coaches can stop at any teachable moment, is simply the best practice organization possible for most teams. There is certainly a place for individual coaching and for drills, but, especially at lower levels, just let them play.

Preparing the Body to Succeed: Pitching Fitness

I love to watch David Wells pitch. He's a fat guy who is still successful. He's working, sweating, breathing hard . . . and he gets people out. Guess what—you're probably not David Wells. Yes, there are pitchers so talented they can win without being physically fit, but those pitchers are not only few and far between, they are giving up an advantage. Just as a good breaking ball or a deceptive motion can help a pitcher, good physical fitness is a tool that every pitcher should have as he walks out to the mound.

The best book about conditioning for pitching remains Tom House's *Fit to Pitch*. There is simply no better researched or complete work on fitness specific to pitching, and I cannot recommend it more highly. While *Fit to Pitch* remains the gold standard, we can add some things to the program to make it even more effective.

The biggest issue I have with most pitching fitness programs is that they tend to ignore the specific skills necessary for pitching while simultaneously ignoring the general skills necessary for athletic success. *Fit to Pitch* clearly has the best base, but again, some exercises can improve that base. I believe strongly in the principles of isometrics, cardiovascular endurance, and explosive power.

Isometrics are quite controversial, but I've never understood why. Certainly there is a place in any fitness program for both traditional weight lifting (also called concentric training) and isometric strength programs. Isometrics, for those unfamiliar, is a system of strength training based on stressing a muscle against an immovable object. Instead of doing a bench press where weight is lifted, isometric variations can be as simple as pushing against a wall.

One of the biggest issues surrounding isometric strength training is the angle variance issue—that is, that benefits accrue only at one angle of effort. As shown above, the idea of the exercise is to stress the muscle against a simulated maximal load,

Any good pitching fitness program includes
proper exercise.

without movement. Studies have shown that the greatest gains
in strength are made at the specific angle where the exercise is
performed. For instance, in one of the figures on page 100, the
athlete's arm is pushing against the wall at a forty-five-degree
angle. Some studies have shown a fifteen-degree variance,
meaning the exercise at forty-five degrees allows gains in the
muscle in a range from thirty to sixty degrees.

The obvious solution to complaints about isometrics is to
perform a series of similar exercises at slightly different angles.
Ideally the angles would simulate a full range of motion for
whatever action is chosen—a typical bench press goes from

zero degrees (full extension) to around 110 degrees (where the bar touches the chest). Understanding this principle in association with the variance principle gives us the knowledge necessary to work any set of muscles completely by using the full range of motion and doing a series of exercises no more than 10 degrees apart. While the variance gives us 15 degrees to work with, the 10-degree mark gives us overlap that increases the work done without adding significant time or strain to the workout.

Some of the most important exercises a pitcher can do are the ones that strengthen the rotator cuff. The Jobe exercises are as follows, in sequence: forward raise, lateral raise, reverse fly, internal rotation, external rotation, "empty can," and upward rotation. More details on these can be found online or in most reputable books on fitness. The exercises described in *Fit to Pitch* or those advocated by Dr. Frank Jobe can also be modified isometrically. In the side-laying abduction, gains can be seen almost immediately. While much of the research done on rotator cuff strengthening is done using lighter weights, typically dumbbells of less than 10 percent of body weight, isometric resistance can increase gains without the risks inherent in the use of a heavier weight.

I cannot overemphasize the importance of using rotator cuff exercises in a pro-active manner. Studies conducted at the Kerlan-Jobe Clinic reveal scary numbers: while 86 percent of athletes see significant results from rotator cuff surgery, 77 percent report continued difficulty throwing and pain with overhead throwing a year after the surgery. Since pitching is an activity with a small window for success—most major league pitchers are between twenty-four and thirty-four years old—losing a year or more to injury has a cumulative effect and can never be regained.

A simple but effective isometric exercise—
pushing against a wall at varying angles.

In fact almost any exercise of use to a pitcher can be modified to use isometrics. Using simple principles of full range of motion, maximal effort, and work at multiple angles, isometric exercises can be a great addition to a training program. One program I have used in the past with pitchers has been to have them continue their normal workouts—often based on *Fit to Pitch*—and add the isometric work as a one- or two-day-a-week "change of pace."

Cardiovascular endurance is also an overlooked element in pitcher fitness. For most pitchers, old-school workout techniques like windsprints or "running poles" make up most of their aerobic work. In fact windsprints are not aerobic to begin with. Using the principles of sport specificity, these kinds of exercises make no sense. Sprints do not translate to any pitching activity, save covering first base. Even with that, they are hardly a straight-line, max-speed activity.

Running poles—a slow jog from foul pole to foul pole—does not translate well either. More akin to the boxing workout of slow jogs that are designed to strengthen the legs for a twelve-round fight, running poles does very little by design and even less when performed at suboptimal levels. Honestly, does any pitcher take this type of running seriously, or do they slog through it, daydreaming?

A better aerobic exercise program would be one that both boosts cardiovascular endurance and focuses on the legs' ability to act continually. If the arms can be added to the routine, all the better. One exercise has everything a pitcher should be looking for, but it will be met with resistance, if not derision, by most coaches and players. Step aerobics is not designed for pitchers but certainly meets every criterion that a pitcher needs. While I don't expect every schoolboy pitcher to slap on legwarmers and "get physical" according to Olivia Newton-John, there are ways to use some of the principles of step aerobics in a more locker-room friendly way. At some point, the pitcher who stops laughing and takes something like step aerobics seriously is going to have an advantage over his opponent.

One drill that both uses a normal pitching workout and involves step aerobics is a simple "play catch" drill. After each throw, the pitcher merely steps up onto a step, then down. Repeat. Another way to bring step aerobics into the pitching workout is to replace the stationary bike often used for conditioning with a simple step aerobic regimen. Not only would it be more effective, it will reduce the cost of many programs. Few Little League teams will have a stationary bike in the dugout; almost everyone will have a step close by.

The final element we can add to the conditioning of pitchers is explosive power. Few exercises attempt to enhance this type of power—the quick bursts of extra-maximal effort that go into pitching. Sprints do this in an extremely small way for the legs, but they do it in a way so nonspecific, and requiring effort so far beyond the benefit, that they are almost counterproductive.

There are better exercises, such as the use of plyometrics for the legs. And for the arms there is a methodology that is gaining traction in America after being used in Europe for years. For simplicity, let's call it "kettlebell training," for the training tool at its core. Again, I will oversimplify these two techniques in describing them. This book is designed to be a broad overview rather than an in-depth look at any specific technique; think of it as a jumping-off point. There are any number of books and videos about plyometrics and a significant number dealing with kettlebell. If performance comes from the sweat of preparation,

Light kettlebells can be used in many range-of-motion exercises.

making you work to get more information is probably a good start.

Kettlebells come in various weights and take their name from their appearance. They have a single, semi-circular handle and vary in size according to their weight. Because of the large handle and properties resulting from the design, they are more easily controlled than standard dumbbells, and they can be substituted for them in most cases. (The opposite is not true: dumbbells cannot be used for most kettlebell exercises.)

For pitchers, light kettlebells can be used in many range-of-motion exercises and in rotator cuff exercises. Remember, though, that it is important never to simulate pitching motions with significant weight. Significant in this case means more than a few pounds. Adding strain to the rotator cuff through weighted deceleration is a risk no pitcher should take with his shoulder.

Kettlebells and their cousin, clubbells, are gaining acceptance in some segments of physical training due to their proven effectiveness. The translation of these tools and their accompanying exercises to baseball and pitching is clear. Again, as with an aerobic program, the lack of wide acceptance gives an athlete who is ahead of the curve an opportunity to gain the advantage.

Beyond physical conditioning programs is the need for physical maintenance. This is seldom discussed in any detail; it is assumed by the schedule of workouts and the implied seasonality of some sports. In today's competitive baseball environment, there is *no* off-season. Physical maintenance includes both diet and nutrition, the fuel for the performance, and recovery and rest.

Nutrition should not be what you buy at the so-called health food store. There is a reason why some food preparations are called supplements: they are designed to supplement a good diet. There are as many plans for proper nutrition, it seems, as there are pills and powders to take. In Miami, Sari Mellman is becoming something new—a nutritionist who does not have a single program for every athlete but who is willing to investigate the particular athlete and develop an individualized program. Athletes such as Tim Brown and Ricky Williams swear by her dietary recommendations. Mellman has a number of baseball clients, none of whom were willing to reveal her secrets!

While Mellman's program is both expensive and exclusive, good basic nutrition does not have to be difficult. Eating a balanced diet, supplemented with vitamins, minerals, and healthy substances such as anti-oxidants, raw foods, and fiber while avoiding things that can be toxic such as drugs, alcohol, and performance-enhancing substances, is simple common sense.

I have purposely chosen not to discuss performance-enhancing drugs—from amphetamines to steroids, from legal, over-the-counter substances like creatine to off-label uses of prescription medications—because the subject is too important to gloss over in this format. Chemical advantages come at too high a cost. Most gains from chemicals are reduced by the lack of underlying work ethic. Players who are looking for chemical shortcuts aren't likely to do extra work in the weight room or on the field.

The advantages gained by pitching properly—using scientifically proven techniques, proper coaching, and common sense—are greater and more lasting than those brought on by chemicals. The 2003 death of Steve Bechler of the Baltimore Orioles is a case in point. Bechler came to spring training overweight, out of shape, and not ready to participate in physical activity in the Florida heat. Instead of putting in the work in the weeks and months before reporting, Bechler tried to take a shortcut, popping metabolism-raising thermogenics in an effort to take the weight off. These so-called thermogenic drugs—essentially uppers—in combination with his physical condition and lack of acclimatization ended in tragedy. Shortcuts sometimes have high costs—you just aren't sure when you'll have to pay. With drug tests proliferating, the risks make even less sense.

The final component of proper conditioning is recovery and rest. This seems simple but can be complex. More than once I have had to explain rest to an athlete. Is rest a short time of doing nothing, or is it a regenerative period when the body is allowed or helped to return from fatigue (a complex concept on its own) to as near full potential as possible?

It's important to understand that rest, whether between workouts or between starts, is completely necessary for effective pitching. All the workouts in the world are rendered meaningless if fatigue reduces the effectiveness of the man on the mound—whether it's the result of too much work, a lack of conditioning, or a hangover. It's important for the pitcher to be placed on the mound with as close to a full "tank of gas" as possible. All members of the pitching team—pitcher, coach, and medical staff—must make sure the pitcher is given that chance.

Recovery is a more complex concept that has to do with muscular damage. Any ballistic work performed by muscles results in some reduced effectiveness, either through microtrauma or chemical changes, such as a buildup of lactic acid. Proper nutrition, supplements, and the techniques of a modern training staff, such as ice, massage, or physical therapy, all assist in muscular recovery. Again, it is up to the pitching team to see that an athlete is given every chance to recover from fatigue and muscular failure.

While not every pitcher will have access to more complex therapy or around-the-clock medical care, as professional athletes do, there is no excuse for not using available resources. Icing after games and workouts is something that is painfully overlooked. I went to a Little League park in Indianapolis and watched as pitchers came out of games. None iced immediately after being removed; many of them remained in the game, so that ice was inappropriate, but only two of sixty-four were observed using ice after the game. While some may have iced when they returned home, the effects were wasted. It is important to ice as quickly as possible after the end of an outing or a workout, with the notable exception that remaining in the game or doing continuing work in practice extends the period of time before icing.

Also, during recovery the arm should not be taxed between starts. Heavy lifting should be avoided, as should nonprogram throwing. While working the arm is important, there are methods to do this safely that we'll discuss later.

For a pitcher, conditioning is paramount. It is a tired cliché, but if a pitcher is a car, conditioning keeps the engine tuned and the fuel tank full. Maintenance of the machine is preferable to a more extensive—and expensive—visit to the mechanic. I'd advise keeping the oil changed, whether you're a Ferrari or a Ford.

Why Work Beats Workload

There's a secret to what Leo Mazzone has been able to do over the past decade in Atlanta. The secret is—well, it's not really a secret. Mazzone is a student of Johnny Sain, the great Boston pitcher who went on to become one of the leading pitching coaches of his day. While much of what is passed down from coach to coach is, at best, worthless information that has been altered slightly by the generational effect of information, Sain's teachings were ahead of their time. Like Earl Weaver, the legendary Baltimore manager, Sain's system worked because somehow he intuitively knew what it took the rest of us decades of research to learn.

Research using some of the latest noninvasive imaging techniques has confirmed Sain's lessons of decades ago: while recovery is extremely important to a pitcher's arm, there is a cycle to the recovery. Inside the cycle of recovery, a stronger, better-conditioned arm recovers more quickly.

In no other activity is an athlete expected to get better by doing less, so why should pitching be that way? Is there any evidence, anecdotal or scientific, that tells us that throwing *less* is better?

Sain had a simple principle: strong arms are better than weak arms. A second principle is even simpler but equally ignored: arms get strong by throwing. The tenets of sport specificity tell us that there are no exercises that perfectly re-create pitching. You have to pitch. Using imaging techniques to monitor the recovery of muscles, it is easy to see where Sain's wisdom comes into play. It is less clear why that wisdom didn't become dogma rather than heresy.

After a pitcher completes a normal outing, his arm is fatigued. It's a natural and necessary occurrence. With this fatigue—which comes at various points depending on a near infinite number of variables—a pitcher begins a cycle of recovery that will restore his mucles in four to five days.

If the day of pitching is day zero, let's look at one cycle of recovery. It is extremely important to note that the level of fatigue is not a binary problem: no pitcher is either fresh or fatigued. There are levels based on last usage, overall usage, conditioning, and recovery profile, among several others, that determine whether a pitcher is effective. Throughout this example we will use a 100-point scale, where 100 is as perfect as our hypothetical pitcher can be physically, and zero is—well, let's just say duct tape is involved. For this scenario, we will assume that a pitcher entered the game as a starter, has a mature arm, and pitched to fatigue. On the scale, he went from 100 to 25.

What does this scale actually tell us, and is it an accurate measure? Surprisingly, the answers are a lot and yes. While it is not ideal, there is quite a bit of research that backs up the concept of biofeedback. If you feel tired, you probably are tired. If you feel good, you probably have the opportunity to pitch well. As a pitching coach, you can use a 0–100 or even a 0–10 scale to get a read on your pitchers. The trick, of course, is that you have to have a positive rapport with your charges that leads to honesty, and you have to know when what you see and what you hear do not match. As a pitcher, you can use either scale to give your coach an idea of where you stand physically. Again, it is imperative that you be honest at all times; the coach has to trust you in order to make the best decision for your team.

On day one, the day after the outing, the pitcher will feel his worst. His arm will feel rubbery and weak, and he will have almost no muscular stamina. There will be some remaining lactic acid in the muscles, and while he could likely make some effective pitches, it's not advisable. Of all days, day one is when a pitcher should take a day off and concentrate on using the appropriate therapeutic techniques. Ice is an important part of the day since there is likely some remnant swelling in the shoulder. This swelling can also be reduced by the use of therapeutic massage. Note that neither of these techniques requires an expert or expensive equipment.

On day two it's important to get some work in. If pitching is possible, it is *always* better to pitch. While a hard workout is not ideal, Mazzone advocates what he calls a "points session." Instead of throwing for velocity, a pitcher during a points session should throw about 60 to 75 percent of maximal effort with a concentration on location. The points Mazzone speaks of are locations: pitching to a specific point in the strike zone or even a specific spot. Having your catcher use a training glove marked with spots or a quadrant can help.

If a pitcher does not have the chance to do a full side session, how can he perform the needed work on day two? First, a mound is not necessary, though it is certainly preferable. Studies have shown that stride length is reduced and the upper body tends to be more upright on flat ground as compared to mound work, so concentration on mechanics is even more important on flat ground. A drill for those who do not have a catcher is to place a paperback book on a tee at the approximate middle of the strike zone. While pitchers joke about the zone being the size of a book, if you can pitch to one, you're already so far ahead of other pitchers that the hitters won't have a chance.

Day two is about working the arm without inducing fatigue. As the arm is recovering, it is important not to stress the system. At 75 percent of maximal effort, much of the stress of pitching is transferred from the muscles to the ligaments. While muscles recover, ligaments are forced to take on a bigger load, one they may or may not be designed to take on. Even with perfect mechanics, fatigue can put too much load on the ligaments.

Still, do not mistake a controlled workout for an excuse not to work. Each side session should work for the pitcher, moving him toward the next start. If control was off in the last outing, working on control during the side session is simple common sense. If there was a mechanical flaw detected, it is important to do some work on correction. The only thing that should not be overtly addressed in a side session is velocity. That will come with muscular recovery and proper mechanical delivery.

Where Mazzone differs from most pitching coaches is in his program for day three. For many, day three is another day to do nothing. At most, many pitchers come in for ice and massage. Instead Mazzone has found that a light workout involving flat ground work and controlled mound work builds the muscles at a time where the muscles are rapidly moving toward full recovery. Instead of impeding the recovery, the light workout serves to reinforce mechanics, build muscular endurance, and keep muscle from binding due to underuse.

On day three pitchers can work with weights. During the season a pitcher should not work to build muscle but to maintain it and build stamina. This is done with lighter weights and increased repetitions. While pitching will work the specific muscles involved, the athlete should concentrate on keeping his whole body healthy and strong.

In this process it is easy to forget that the legs are recovering at the same time the pitching arm is recovering. The legs do not feel as fatigued since they are often much stronger and have significantly more stamina than the arm does. Even using proper mechanics, the legs are never used at a maximal level during an outing. Still, it is important to give the legs time and assistance in recovery and to work the legs in any conditioning program.

By day three the pitcher should be back to 75 or 80 on the perceived fatigue scale. If asked to pitch, he probably could do so effectively. We see this almost every year in the playoffs, where a pitcher is asked to return on two days' rest for an inning or two. (We're not talking here about relief pitchers—a whole different ball game.) While the pitcher can perform for a short period of time—perhaps longer due to the adrenaline that comes with the situation—he will immediately return to the cycle of recovery. Used on short rest, a pitcher must return immediately to his off-day program and listen closely to his body.

A great deal of controversy surrounds day four. Since the early 1970s, most teams have used a five-man rotation, meaning that each pitcher receives four or five days between starts, depending on the scheduling of off-days. The fifth pitcher can occasionally be skipped depending on schedule, in order to give the top of the rotation more opportunity. Before this scheme, the four-man rotation was the order of the day.

In work done by the tireless Dr. Rany Jazayerli of Baseball Prospectus, he branded the five-man rotation with a tag it rightly deserves: failure. Nowhere else in baseball is it so painfully obvious that the game in general knows next to nothing about how to save its own pitchers. While the five-man rotation was designed to reduce stress on pitchers and result in fewer injuries, in fact the opposite has been true. It is not the five-man rotation per se that creates weaker, more injury-prone arms; rather, it is the mind-set surrounding the five-man, and a failure to understand the benefits of the four-man.

Surprisingly, one of the greatest beneficiaries of the four-man rotation in modern baseball, Jim Palmer, is against the idea of its return. When I asked Palmer why he thought it wasn't used currently, he said, "It has no place. These young pitchers can't handle the things we did. All this pitch-count nonsense and . . . you know why there are so many injuries these days? MRI. We just pitched through that kind of stuff." I came to understand why Palmer and his manager, Earl Weaver, were often on each other's nerves.

The five-man rotation was inaugurated in 1982 by the Los Angeles Dodgers and was not, in fact, rolled out to protect arms. The Dodgers simply had five, perhaps six, good starters, including Don Sutton and Tommy John. Instead of protecting arms, the five-man shifted some of the workload (defined by games started) from the top of the rotation to the bottom. Dr. Jazayerli provides the numbers:

Slot	Games Started			Cumulative		
	1973	1999	Diff	1973	1999	Diff
1	37.3	33.2	−4.1	37.3	33.2	−4.1
2	34.1	30.7	−3.4	71.4	63.9	−7.5
3	29.6	28.3	−1.3	101.0	92.2	−8.8
4	23.2	23.6	+0.4	124.2	115.8	−8.4
5	14.9	17.9	+3.0	139.1	133.7	−5.4
6+	22.8	28.2	+5.4	161.9	161.9	0

(The cumulative numbers add up to only 161.9 because of a few rainouts.)

By using a five-man rotation, we've robbed the ace of four starts and handed them over to a guy who, for most of baseball history, would be in the bullpen. As expected, Jazayerli also found that this plan didn't make the rotation more effective. ERA has risen from 3.31 to 3.51. While the offensive explosion might be blamed for this increase, relative to the rest of the league it is an accurate reflection of less effective pitching.

The apparent problem with the four-man rotation is the greater pitching workload. "If the ace gets more work, he'll break down more often," many argue. In fact, a simple adjustment to the philosophy of rotation management is all that's necessary to make this work and to make baseball better and safer.

A four-man rotation should be used in combination with strictly controlled limits, either pitch counts or one of the more scientific methods we will discuss later. Jazayerli argues that not only does using a four-man improve the rotation, but by pulling the starter earlier it creates pinch-hitting opportunities that can slightly improve an offense (in a non-DH league).

How then does a four-man rotation work with the idea of increasing workload during recovery? Instead of throwing on the side on day four in a highly controlled manner, the pitcher instead goes to the mound. Knowing he will pitch only until he reaches a predetermined cutoff point, the pitcher is forced to be efficient in order to go deep into a game, and will be subject to less seasonal fatigue, the type that builds over the course of a season and reduces the cyclic peaks.

At many levels, workload is not closely monitored. The pitch counts I have seen at some high schools and colleges borders on criminal negligence. Boyd Nation, a leading collegiate baseball writer, has done amazing and disturbing work on the workloads inflicted on top college pitchers and has documented the breakdowns caused by this abuse, all in the name of winning a meaningless game. It is one thing to ask your ace to pitch on short rest or an extended pitch count during the penultimate game of the College World Series; it is quite another to leave a major-league-quality pitcher on the mound for 140 pitches against Podunk U. in the middle of March.

The writer Alex Belth, a New York native, wrote a lyrical piece about walking home from a game at Yankee Stadium and seeing a teenager throwing a tennis ball against an alley wall, fielding it, then throwing it. Stopping to have a catch, Alex remembered the simple joys of throwing a ball and talking to a new friend. On a warm late-summer day, there's almost nothing better than the rhythm and power of a ball slapping into your pal's glove. It disturbed Belth, however, that the kid he met was alone, and was surprised that Alex would even want to play catch.

There was a time when kids would play sandlot baseball until their mothers had to drag their grass-stained butts home as the sun slid down behind the horizon. I haven't seen a kid playing catch outside a baseball field in years. The world is different today, but with change comes consequence. Until we regain the concept that a pitcher gets better by pitching, that an arm gets stronger by throwing, and that putting your best pitcher on the mound is usually better than putting your worst out there, we're all missing something beautiful.

The Secret Weapon: Stretching Your Concept of Stretching

Within the realm of baseball and baseball statistics, there are always outliers. These numbers or players that are so far outside the realm of normal performance that they either reset the bar we judge by or we merely marvel at them and seek to explain them. When Mark McGwire tore past Roger Maris's venerated single-season home run record, few expected those seventy homers to last only a few years atop the charts.

For pitchers, outliers exist in several realms. One popular but fatally flawed statistical study attempted to take a different look at how pitchers fit inside the game. It took responsibility away from the man on the mound and recast him as a victim of random chance who hoped that his defense would save him from hits. Any person who has pitched knows this is untrue, and better analysts have taken apart the theory on paper as well. One of the study's biggest holes was its failure to explain the different situation of knuckleballers. In the end, knucklers became the outliers that anyone who's seen one pitch knows are very real.

While knucklers are an obvious outlier, there are others. What makes Randy Johnson such a devastating pitcher despite the mechanical challenges his height poses? What kept Nolan Ryan healthy and throwing in the high nineties as he was approaching fifty years of age? How do Rickey Henderson and Barry Bonds not lose any of their effectiveness—perhaps getting better—as they age? How do some pitchers absorb workloads that would put a normal pitcher on the first flight to see Dr. Jim Andrews?

The easy answer is to call them mysteries. Freaks. But we won't get good answers to the question of what keeps players healthy if we continue to take the easy way out. While there are likely answers in the realm of genetics or in complex patterns that we lack sample size to see, there is one distinct point of similarity, one important enough to take seriously.

When asked how he stayed healthy through a baseball career that now spans four decades and does not include a single major injury, Rickey Henderson responded, "It's a little bit of luck, some good stuff from my mama, and I have a commitment to stretching." This commitment to stretching is common among athletes who have long careers and avoid the disabled list. While it is not yet common enough to point to as a cure-all, it does have enough benefits to point others toward it.

The problem is the word "stretching." To most of us, especially inside the world of baseball, stretching is the same set of calisthenics that we loafed through before practices. Toe touches, hurdler's stretches, and windmills are better than nothing, but not much better, especially when performed in a halfhearted manner. While a commitment to basic stretches would be an improvement, just as a commitment to fitness is better than nothing, an almost unknown system is available that some elite pitchers use like a secret weapon.

While the sports machines of Communist East Germany and the Soviet Union have been dismantled and in some ways discredited, some of their advances have not yet been widely disseminated in the West. Outside of some of their illegal chemical work, the methods used by the Russians could be applied in baseball for gains that would give the practitioners an advantage in strength, flexibility, and injury avoidance. For stretching, there is no better system I know of than the one called "Clasp Knife," advocated by Pavel Tsatsouline.

Tsatsouline's system is neither simple nor easy. It may be among the more painful exercise systems I have ever seen or participated in. Based on anatomical principles and advanced kinesiological concepts, Clasp Knife can create dramatic gains in flexibility in a relatively short period of time, given a better-than-average motivation and pain tolerance. Like the more widely used Proprioceptive Neuromuscular Facilitation (say that three times fast, or just call it PNF), Clasp Knife concentrates on using the body's reflexes to go past the point of resistance. Where it differs from PNF is that Clasp Knife focuses on increasing strength in the muscles and adding flexibility to the joints.

Typical stretching is often ineffective, even when done properly, because it seeks to do the wrong thing. As an example, let's look at stretching the muscle most often injured in the game of baseball, the hamstring. Most baseball players, if asked to stretch their hamstring, do a straight-legged bend. Most strength coaches and trainers would have their athlete perform a series of assisted stretches, usually a straight-leg, self-powered stretch. While these can be effective, they are not as effective as the Clasp Knife method. Studies show that techniques similar to Clasp Knife can be 267 percent more effective than static stretching.

The method is simple if not easy. I invite you to try it after I describe the method. Stand and bend forward from the waist, much as you would for a typical straight-leg hamstring stretch. Allow your body to hang forward, but if there is tension/stress in your lower back, bend your knees slightly until you feel that tension leave your back. Your hands and arms should hang loosely and relaxed, pointing to the ground. At normal muscular tension, most athletes will find their hands at a level just above the midpoint of their tibia (shinbone).

To start the stretch, instead of relaxing or using an antagonist muscle to attempt to lengthen the target muscle, we'll use the muscle and its processes to lengthen itself. Contract the hamstring, where you feel the contraction most in the belly of the muscle, located at just below the midpoint. Isolate the contraction to the hamstring. If you feel a contraction in the hip flexors, you'll want to add a bit more flexion to your knees. If you have difficulty getting a good contraction in your hamstrings, you can also flex your glutes (butt). The force used should be a near maximal isometric contraction. Hold the contraction until fatigue sets in and you can feel the contraction losing force or the muscle begins to struggle. At this point, release the contraction and you'll feel yourself drop farther than before. In tests with high school athletes that had never used Clasp Knife before, the first stretch after contraction is about three inches farther than before contraction.

Three inches may not sound like much, but this is a significant and immediate result. And it's only the first step. We're not done. After a brief, fifteen-to-thirty-second rest period, begin a second isometric contraction in the hamstring. Again, if necessary, involve the glutes or add flexion to the knees in order to maintain isolation on the intended muscle. As you release this contraction, you'll feel an increased drop. In tests with high school athletes, the second post-contraction stretch went an additional two inches, or a total of five inches in just over one minute of work.

With this exercise, because of the involvement of the ligaments of the back, it is extremely important not simply to rise up at the hips. Instead, squat slightly until the back is nearer to vertical, then raise yourself up. The old "lift with your legs, not with your back" holds true. Flexibility is not a plus when it comes to the spine.

With each additional maximal contraction there is diminishing return from the additional work. The sequence of contraction, extension, and rest should be continued until there is no discernible increased drop over two or three extensions. But there is also a benefit over time, meaning that the starting point of the extension at the next workout tends to be lower than the original starting point. Over a continuous period of time, using the Clasp Knife method, the initial extension will continue to be longer and the overall flexibility of joints will be greater. The Clasp Knife also will help increase strength through the isometric contractions and the ability of the muscles to contract through a larger range of motion.

As I noted in the section on fitness for pitching, isometric contractions are one of the best ways to train in season. Clasp Knife stretching takes this a step further, increasing strength and pairing it with flexibility and increased range of motion. Moreover, it does it in a way that makes these often separate activities mesh in something that works out to be greater than the sum of its parts. Just as the pitching motion is the body working in a kinetic chain, Clasp Knife stretching appears to work holistically.

Additional Clasp Knife stretches can be found in Tsatsourine's books, *Super Joints* and *Relax into Stretch*, but all work on the same principles of isometric contraction, then relaxation into an extension. Lengthening the muscles rather than pulling the tendons like taffy is a much safer and more effective method. But it's not easy or comfortable or even intuitive, meaning that there will be significant player resistance to the technique despite results.

Putting the Tubes Away

Taking the isometric strength training and Clasp Knife stretching one step further, we should look closely at one of the more popular pitching exercises and determine where—or even if—it fits into a well-designed pitching program. Over the past fifteen years, many pitchers have been instructed to use flexible surgical tubing to provide resistance in their range-of-motion drills.

There is no doubt that resistance training can be effective, but as with any exercise it poses questions beyond mere efficacy. Is the use of surgical tubing the best method of resistance training for pitchers? Is it the most cost-effective method? Most important, what are the alternatives?

There is nothing inherently negative in the use of surgical tubing as part of a pitcher's workout. There are simply methods that are more effective. If someone feels strongly about the continued use of tubing, it's not something worth fighting over. In the battle to save pitchers from damage and make them more effective, this isn't the place to focus your attention. Even the most backward of pitching coaches seldom get angry when someone does more than they ask.

The idea behind the use of surgical tubing is to provide resistance throughout the normal pitching motion. Where tubing fails is in not providing sufficient resistance, and possibly altering the pitching motion. Any resistance training that does not directly relate to the pitching motion is at best wasted and at worst counterproductive. It is much more important to provide resistance through the pitching motion without alteration to normal, efficient mechanics.

Strength training, by its own definition, uses maximum possible resistance in order to tax muscle fiber. The maximum resistance has to be the one that *can't* be lifted! By taking the idea of surgical tube resistance and introducing isometric principles into the action, the pitcher will achieve significantly better gains while maintaining the integrity of his pitching motion.

The only downside to using an isometric element is, as we said before, that isometric exercises provide muscle gain only at the length and angle where resistance is met. Unlike tube exercises, using an isometric element requires a longer period of time and a complete series of resistance at as many possible angles as can be made. While anything that takes more time may tax a workout, I think most any pitcher or pitching coach would rather put in more time and get a better result. If not, their goals really need to be questioned.

There are many ways to introduce the isometric element, but the simplest is a nonflexible cord or even a towel. At each point in the delivery, as if we had twenty or thirty pictures of a pitcher going through his delivery in sequence, stop and pull against the cord with maximum force. A buddy will hold the other end. Try to make it so that your arm does not change position through the ten-to-fifteen-second contraction. It is possible to tie the cord to a fence or other stationary object, but you will need to alter your foot position to remove slack from the cord.

While twenty to thirty positions is a reasonable number, doing more—in essence, getting resistance at every joint angle and muscle length in the delivery—is ideal. As I've said before, doing more is seldom a negative.

A number of normal pitching exercises can easily be adapted to include an isometric element. All it takes is a little common sense, some ingenuity, and the knowledge that there is only one perfect motion for each pitcher. Increasing strength and flexibility within that motion will only make the pitcher better.

Another way to add an element strength and neuromuscular coordination to this drill is to introduce what therapists call "perturbation." Perturbation is an attempt to move the arm (or any body part) from the isometric position through the use of multidirectional forces. In therapy the arm would be tapped in a random fashion while the patient attempts to hold the arm in the static position. The perturbations will move the arm slightly, and the muscles will be forced to compensate in order to return the arm to the starting position. If a partner is not available, doing isometrics against a "shaky" but strong platform can help. A great tool for this is a chain link fence. Rather

Another simple isometric exercise, using a nonflexible cord or towel and pulling it at various points in the pitcher's delivery.

than doing isometrics against a wall, using the chain link introduces a slight perturbation but is sturdy enough to provide sufficient resistance. Variety keeps workouts from getting stale, both for the muscles and the mind.

Finally we should discuss a technique that is one of the more apparent skills in baseball, was first documented in the 1920s, yet is seldom if ever discussed or taught. Most pitching coaches at any level will tell you that this principle is both a key to great pitching and something that happens naturally in great pitchers. While the former is true, the latter is not.

Look into the face of a great pitcher as he stares down a dangerous batter and you will often see nothing—no change in features, no change in demeanor, and certainly no tension. This same skill applies to Michael Jordan taking a last-second shot or Peyton Manning dropping back to pass. First described by Dr. Edmund Jacobsen in his 1934 book *You Must Relax*, the practice of controlling tension in noninvolved muscles, especially those of the face and hands, where the body has a greater number of nerves, has proven to be both important and teachable. Barry Zito, the Cy Young lefty, said in an interview with Dan Patrick of ESPN that "throwing in the ninth is no harder than the first or second. I just take a deep breath and feel all the tension go out of me. Then I throw a strike." Zito possesses one of the more devastating breaking balls in modern baseball, but it is his ability to relax and rely on his repeatable mechanics that allow that pitch to come across the plate in crucial situations with a break that has been measured at better than twenty inches.

While there are as many techniques for relaxation as there are pitchers who need to learn the skill, I don't believe any one technique will work for everyone. Relaxation, unlike the pitching motion, is not based on Newtonian laws. Each pitcher must find his own path to relax himself effectively and remove the antagonistic or wasted energies from his pitching. While Rick Peterson will discuss Zen philosophies, Leo Mazzone will talk about pitching confidently. These are just two ways of saying what Jacobsen said seventy years ago: to pitch effectively, you must relax.

Facing the Enemy: What Is Fatigue?

In the war to save pitchers, there are many enemies—ignorance, overuse, and the warrior mentality of competitive sports—but the most serious of battles must be waged against one insidious yet harmless-sounding foe: fatigue.

Inside the muscles during any workout, there is both a constructive and a deconstructive effect. Anyone who has completed even the most basic of workouts has left feeling tired, as if their arms cannot lift a pillow or they can't lift their legs. The next day can often be worse as pain and soreness, along with reduced range of motion due to swelling and pain reflex, makes one question his desire to return to the gym or to the mound. Even so, few understand the processes that cause the reactions we refer to generally as fatigue. We look again to science to "take us inside" the muscles, using both simple biology and more technologically advanced imaging that almost literally lets us look inside the body as its processes happen.

Since most of the research in this field focuses on lifting weight, something much easier to re-create in the lab than an activity like pitching, we will explore it. Any muscular activity is the same physically and chemically, allowing us to translate the results from one activity to another with confidence. A muscle reacts to lifting weights just as it does to pitching.

Weight lifting consists of two distinct phases of work. The concentric phase is the portion of any lift where the bulk of the weight is lifted, such as the upward push on the bar during a bench press. The eccentric phase is the return portion of the lift, such as the downward lowering of the bar during a bench press. Both portions of the lift contribute to both the muscle gain and the muscle damage seen during resistance exercises.

The eccentric portion of any activity is a form of forced lengthening of the muscle. Forced lengthening with high weight loads causes microscopic tears in the small fibers that make up the muscle and the connective tissues. These eccentric contractions usually involve fewer muscle fibers than other contractions. With fewer fibers involved, each individual muscle fiber is forced to do more work and take more physical damage.

The reverse of this is the concentric portion of the activity. While the individual muscle fibers take less accepted load due to their increased involvement, it requires much more metabolic activity and resources. This activity quickly leads to depletion of muscle energy stores such as ATP and glycogen (yes, Atkins devotees, it's a carbohydrate). This exercise-induced depletion can lead to greater susceptibility to fibrous damage.

As the muscle cells begin their recovery from work, they must deal with both the microtrauma and necessary repairs as well as normal chemical imbalances. Normally calcium will increase and activate enzymes, including the proteins necessary to generate powerful contractions. The calcium also builds up in the mitochondria, the "powerhouse" of the cell. This excess calcium slows the energy production within the cell—the body's method of slowing down the muscle, giving it time to recover.

As all these changes take place at the cellular level, the body begins to make more macro-level changes. Fluid begins to rush into the area, bringing with it the body's "fix it" crew—macrophages, neutrophils, and similar immune cells—to the site of the trauma. There is a negative aspect to the activity of the cleanup: some research indicates that without intervention, a compound called free radicals can build up. Thus it's important that early in the recovery an athlete should eat foods or supplements rich in anti-oxidants. The body also has a more difficult time converting carbohydrates into energy as it recovers, making even seemingly small dietary changes important.

In addition to cellular and systemic changes, some functional changes are important to understand in order to help the body recover properly. For a pitcher on a normal schedule, any slowing of the recovery process can have consequences on the mound. Studies that have used weight lifting as their muscular stressor show that strength in affected muscles is diminished for between one and three days. The strength normally recovers on a predictable curve, coming back to a *usable* level quickly but not back to full strength before as much as fourteen days have passed. For a pitcher, this could mean that instead of going back out at 100 percent, he will be coming out at 95 percent.

One of the most visible signs of muscle stress and recovery is swelling. This is the result of the previously mentioned delivery of immune cells. Along with increased blood flow during and immediately after a workout—what bodybuilders call "the pump"—fluid accumulation will normally last three to four days. Normal muscle soreness and decreased range of motion are the result. Some recent studies indicate that soreness may also be the result of increased sensitivity in the nerves in and around the muscles. It is important to remember there is a big difference between soreness and pain, and that baseball does not allow crying.

The muscle is also depleted as well as damaged. The fuel for muscles, provided by the glucose transport system, slowly recovers over a period of four days, but it is drastically slowed in the first forty-eight hours. It is important to keep the body provided with proper foods and nutrients, but not to try to force-feed the system. While all this sounds ugly, it is simply the body's defense and rebuilding system. By the time fourteen days have passed, the immune system has finished its work, the muscle is completely replenished, and muscle fibers are not only repaired, but bigger and stronger.

What's that? You have four days between starts, not fourteen? A starting pitcher expends nearly the same energy as a runner during a ten-kilometer run, and he is expected to do this thirty times or more in a season. Keeping the body as healthy as possible becomes not just helpful but imperative. While it is nearly impossible to accelerate healing and recovery, it is quite possible to avoid putting unnecessary obstacles in your path. The cycle of tearing down a muscle that is not fully recovered prevents pitchers from gaining significant muscle mass due to the muscular work of pitching.

Since pitchers do not have time to allow full recovery, they must note the signs of excessive muscular damage and work with their coach and medical team to ensure that the body doesn't cross the line from "not at full strength" to "breaking down." Since no one knows his body better than the athlete himself, it is extremely important to be honest, both with your coach and with yourself. A pitcher is no good to his team if he can't throw.

In addition to listening to your body, there are other signs to look for, such as making sure that full range of motion has returned, that muscle strength is at or near normal. One of the best tests is muscle size. With a simple tape measure around the belly of the muscle, it is easy to determine if the muscle is still in the process of recovery. While a pitcher will still be sore the day after a start, with proper medical care and an enlightened approach to recovery there is no reason why he cannot retain an effective pitching arm.

Techniques that help the process of recovery include massage (to increase blood flow and reduce swelling), use of therapeutic modalities such as hot or cold whirlpools, compression, and simple icing. Of course these should always be done properly and under the direction and supervision of qualified athletic trainers or doctors.

When it comes to measuring fatigue, perception seems to mirror reality. Several studies have shown that accurate descriptions of muscular fatigue have a high correlation to the results of imaging studies, especially thermography. While few pitchers have such high-tech equipment at their disposal, much of its value can be replicated by self-awareness and a coach who asks the right questions.

Fatigue is the enemy, allowing all that a pitcher has worked hard to build to fall away. Fatigue not only tears down the body, it breaks down technique and breaks down the mind. Pitchers who can successfully manage their inevitable fatigue will be healthy, effective, and ultimately winners.

The Advent of Prehab

One of the most exciting developments in the past fifteen years is a concept that has come to be known as "prehab," a term coined and trademarked by Tom House in *1984* and popularized by a team at the American Sports Medicine Institute led by Dr. Glenn Fleisig, and by pitching coach Rick Peterson. Peterson's results with the Oakland A's are impeccable. In 2002 and 2003 the A's, as a system, had almost *no* pitcher arm injuries.

As Peterson's results have been noticed across baseball, other teams are slowly buying into the concepts of prehab, either by working with Fleisig's Alabama-based team or by trying to reinvent the wheel.

The principles behind prehab are simple. First, it is easier to prevent than rehabilitate. Second, it is easier to teach than correct. Finally, it is a system of all or nothing: without a complete buy-in from all stakeholders, the system quickly breaks down. In Oakland, as detailed wonderfully in the best-selling book *Moneyball* by Michael Lewis, the entire organization is run by one man. That man is General Manager Billy Beane, universally acknowledged as one of the smartest men in baseball but also a tempestuous force of nature. Either through guile or force, Beane controls every aspect of Oakland's baseball operations at every level.

As described in ASMI's research, Fleisig and his team have broken pitching into its component parts and worked on the kinetics and kinematics of the whole motion. Most of this work is done using high-speed cameras, sophisticated and technical measurement devices, and the best available research techniques and tools.

While it seems to be easier to prevent injuries than to repair them, injury can occur in so many different ways that it is difficult to prevent in the context of the game. It is a fact that a pitcher would likely never be injured if he used an ideal biomechanical motion and received adequate rest between outings to return him to full strength. But the game as constructed does not allow for this, so prehab seeks to operate under realistic conditions.

Fatigue, of course, is the biggest enemy of any pitcher. Using the principles of prehab, a pitcher is prepared before the season using strength, flexibility, and biomechanical training.

During the season the pitcher uses sound scientific principles to recover after efficient, monitored outings and is given the proper care and nutrition during the recovery period. The key here is the definition of "efficient, monitored outings." Again, we go back to the idea of a pitcher working on strict limits, determined either by pitches or velocity.

If a pitcher is removed from a game before he reaches complete muscle failure—in this case defined as the point where mechanics break down and the shoulder and elbow become stressed—he will be able to recover more quickly. As we've shown, pitchers who recover in forty-eight hours are more effective than those who require seventy-two hours or longer. Removing a pitcher too soon is always preferable to removing him too late. A pitching coach or manager should almost always go with his first instinct to remove a pitcher from a game. If the pitcher shows signs of fatigue in his pitches, motion, or mannerisms, by removing him the coach is not only saving that pitcher from potential problems, but saving his team as well.

Certainly there are arguments to be made that 80 percent of a team's ace is better than 100 percent of a pitcher in the pen. But if that's true, the coach hasn't spent enough time with his bullpen pitchers and has failed to put the team in a position to win. Perhaps he leaves the ace in, but instead of being 80 percent, he's 60 percent or lower. Perhaps the pitcher doesn't recover as quickly and is worse the next game. The only time a pitcher should be allowed to go beyond the preset limit is if there is to be a period of enforced and extended rest following the outing. I'm not going to tell anyone they shouldn't—within reason—throw everything but the kitchen sink out there in game seven or a state championship game. But remember, each pitch now may be one fewer pitch later.

Pitchers often say they "come back stronger" after surgery. This is always false. A pitcher will feel like he's throwing harder because he became accustomed to throwing with reduced velocity as his injury progressed. It's quite possible that some, if not many, major league pitchers have never been at 100 percent. Much of the improvement they will see is attributable to the forced work of rehab.

Had these pitchers worked as hard at keeping their arm healthy before surgery, most would have never needed it! I call this Tommy's paradox, a reference to Tommy John. It never ceases to amaze me that the pitchers who were lazy and wouldn't correct obvious mechanical flaws are often the hardest workers once they are faced with the end of their career. An old commercial about oil filters said, "Pay me now or pay me later." If the choice for a pitcher is working hard now or working hard after a surgeon has worked on him, I don't understand why anyone wouldn't prefer rehab.

Concentrating on strength, flexibility, stamina, mechanics, and recovery are steps any pitcher, any team, at any level can do now with little or no expense, added equipment, or change to their system. Following scientifically sound principles within almost any throwing program will add gains. Following the best throwing programs, such as those advocated by Tom House or Mike Marshall, will increase the effectiveness of any pitcher or staff. This commitment to prehab will save not only pitchers but lost time and money.

For pitching coaches, the final step to a prehab program is the collection of information. Rick Peterson has sent both his A's and Mets pitchers to Glenn Fleisig at the American Sports Medicine Institute for analysis under the lenses of high-speed cameras. This isn't accessible to many individuals or teams due to time and cost, but establishing a baseline doesn't require a team of scientists. It requires time, effort, and a good eye. It would probably help to take notes and, if possible, do some video. Here's a checklist for a coach to follow:

What does his motion look like?
What flaws do I see?
What pitches does he throw?
What velocity does he have?
Does he control his pitches?
Can he locate his pitches?
Is his motion consistent?
What are three keys I see in his delivery?
What does the catcher see?
What does the batter see?

Yes, the last two questions require the coach to get behind the plate or to stand in against his pitcher. No one said you wouldn't get dirty when you took on the responsibilities of coaching.

You can certainly collect more data about pitchers with advanced equipment and tests. But they are not essential. Establishing a prehab program actually doesn't require much at all beyond a commitment. Think back to Stan Conte who said that the Giants reduced injuries because they decided to do so. There's no reason your team cannot do the same.

9

THE PITCHING WORKLOAD

Pitching Statistics and Pitch Counts

At the mention of math, many baseball players' eyes glaze over. Worse, they turn hostile. Curt Schilling, a former Cy Young winner, has taken public exception to those he derisively calls "statheads sucking the life out of the game." Elsewhere, people inside and outside the game look at the numbers generated by the statisticians who swarm the game of baseball and sneer. The best-seller *Moneyball* met resistance in baseball circles because it committed the heresy of suggesting there might be a better way.

Paul DePodesta, now the Dodgers' general manager, in a landmark speech to a gathering of financial professionals, discussed what he calls the "naive question." This question is, "If we started fresh, would we do things the way we do them now?" DePodesta is committed to analyzing and changing the processes used to address the game of baseball and the problem of winning games with a limited budget.

Out of desperation and intelligence, the Oakland A's pioneered the use of statistical methods in putting together a baseball team.

But their key finding was that they were often either fooled by what they saw or not able to see everything they would like. No one man can see every game pitched. No man can see the pitching motion the way a high-speed camera can. Most parents cannot be at every practice or even every game their child plays. But this is no excuse for not monitoring every major and minor leaguer or for not being able to understand if your child's coaches are doing their best to protect his arm.

Instead we are forced to journey into the world of statistics. From a simple pitch count or box score to more advanced sabermetric measures, it is no longer a question of resistance to stats—it is a question of competence. Writer Dayn Perry's famous "beer and tacos" article—in which he argues for scouting *and* statistics—holds completely true in this case. Failing to understand the new statistics and the concepts surrounding them is endangering our pitchers.

All too many of the coaches guiding our pitchers today are equipped with a skill set that does not include all it should. While this has largely been because of resistance by "old-school" baseball, it is also a problem of presentation. Understanding statistics should not be intimidating and should never make you feel like you're back in sophomore algebra class. While many of these statistics were developed by minds honed at MIT or Stanford, *you* don't have to do the number crunching. While some of you may be interested in polynomials, correlations, or the finer points of Excel, it is more than enough simply to know where to find these new measures and how to apply them.

Counting is not new. Since the invention of Arabic numerals and the concept of zero, no sport has absorbed numbers into the fabric of its spirit more gleefully than baseball. One of its pioneers, Alexander Cartwright, codified the statistics of the game according to the principles and morality of his time, seeing in batting average and fielding percentage a way to glimpse the soul of a man.

Under the guidance of the Society for American Baseball Research (SABR) and several leading researchers, baseball statistics have recently undergone a rebirth. Although they were often conceived in an era when the best tools were a slide rule and a love for the game, they have been remade in the image of the computer age.

In pitching, statistics have seldom given us the true measure of a pitcher. The most widely used yardsticks—wins, earned run average (ERA), and saves—are among the least telling in the game. The statistic called "win" tells us less about a particular pitcher and more about the way early baseball looked at the game. The pitcher who is in the game when his team takes the lead—which they do not relinquish—earns a win. Note this: it's the team that takes the lead, not the pitcher. The noted writer and statistician Lee Sinins says about the "win" statistic: "Wins and losses are an arcane bookkeeping measure. I can assure you that if I, Bill James, Pete Palmer, Keith Woolner, Joe Sheehan, or any other sabermetrician had been the one who came up with it, we'd be laughed at, not just by the rest of the sabermetric community but by the media as well. The only reason why the stat is still there is because it is entrenched in the culture. But that doesn't make it any more right than the inequality of women, which had also been entrenched in our culture."

Why not use the traditional earned run average to determine how well a pitcher performed? Good statistics isolate a performance. While a defense as porous as Swiss cheese certainly hurts any pitcher, it remains the pitcher's sole function to prevent runs from scoring. New attempts have been made to isolate pitching statistics from run support, defense, and park effects, and it is these statistics that offer a truer measure of performance.

In the eyes of many experts, the save stat is the worst of the usual yardsticks. Invented in the 1960s, it is perhaps the only statistic that has changed the way certain players are used. It is not fair to give the statistic or its inventor, Jerome Holtzman, the full blame or full credit. The age of the specialty pitcher was on its way by the time Holtzman codified a reward. Pitchers in the sixties like Luis Arroyo, Ryne Duren, and Dick Radatz were being used as late-inning specialists but still did not have the cachet or respect of starters. With the seventies came Bruce Sutter, Goose Gossage, and a flood of pitchers who closed out games. By the eighties the true "closer" concept was born, and pitchers like Trevor Hoffman and Dennis Eckersley were used *only* in save situations.

By definition, a save occurs when a pitcher finishes a game with the tying run on base or scheduled to bat during the final inning. In 2003 Cy Young winner Eric Gagne was seldom used in a nonsave situation on his way to fifty-five saves. Years earlier Bill James had done a study attempting to determine if this pattern of usage was in fact the most effective way to use a relief ace. It is important to note that James did not attempt to debunk the myth of the closer, nor did he embrace a concept that came to be known as "closer by committee," a scheme tied to him in his association with the 2003 Boston Red Sox.

According to James, the best use of a relief ace—the best pitcher available in the bullpen on any given day—is in a tie game in the seventh or eighth inning: "Use your best guy when you're in the seventh inning and tied or up by one run. You can also use your best guy late in tie games if he's not tired." You'll note that there's no mention of a committee here. You might infer from James's statements that any number of relievers could be used in defined save situations, but that idea was not key to the study. Instead we must look to another new tool in the arsenal of modern baseball analysis to determine if James's study holds true in what can arguably be called the greatest season by a reliever (Gagne) in baseball history.

An offshoot of Bill James's work in the early eighties is Retrosheet, a nonprofit research work whose aim is to collect detailed play-by-play data from every professional baseball game ever played. Seldom has a task been as married to the abilities of technology as Retrosheet or its predecessor, Project Scoresheet. Combining the powers of modern databases, the Internet, and the tireless research of volunteers, Retrosheet has collected an amazing—but not yet complete—database that can be searched, queried, and mined for priceless information. Using data from Retrosheet and proprietary work from Baseball

Prospectus, we can reconstruct the season of Eric Gagne. Blake Kirkman, my research assistant on this book, did the heavy lifting on this topic and came up with his own way of analyzing pitchers.

Eric Gagne—A Study of (Near) Perfection

To say that Eric Gagne's adjective-inducing 2003 performance was just another season would be akin to the notion that the Beatles were just another rock band. The fact is that Gagne's season's performance was one for the ages.

Traditional metrics alone, such as his 55 saves and 1.20 ERA, showed enough to make the goggle-wearing Dodger closer the choice for the National League Cy Young Award. Gagne further impressed by striking out an astronomical 137 batters in only 82.3 innings. Further proof of his superior performance was his limiting opponents to a .133 batting average.

As is most often the case, traditional metrics prove to be only the tip of the iceberg in discussing Gagne's season. For all his strikeouts and saves, the bottom line may best be seen in the fact that Gagne was the best reliever in baseball in terms of preventing runs. His 32.6 Adjusted Runs Prevented, based on the analysis of Michael Wolverton at Baseball Prospectus, indicates that Gagne prevented approximately 33 runs more than what would have been prevented by the average major league reliever during the course of his specific 82.3 innings pitched. This calculates to an incredible difference of 3.6 runs per every nine innings pitched.

Similarly impressive, though admittedly less complex, it can be shown that Gagne saved the Dodgers just under 23 runs versus what the team's starting rotation would have individually allowed had the starters remained in the games they started.

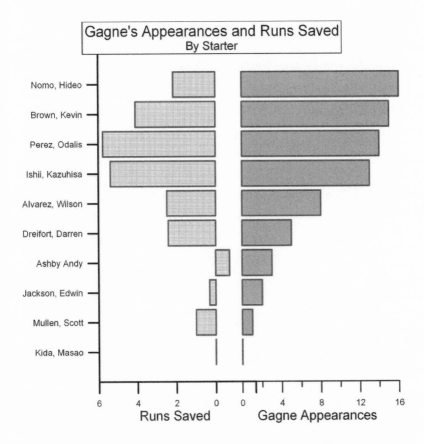

This calculation can be figured by determining the average number of runs allowed by each starting pitcher on the Los Angeles staff, numbers that are also readily available from Wolverton and Baseball Prospectus. As can be seen on the chart, Gagne appeared most often in games started by Hideo Nomo, 16 in all. Through those 16 appearances, Gagne saved the Dodgers 2.406 runs over what Nomo would have allowed, on average, in the same number of innings pitched.

The Dodger pitcher who received the most help from Gagne's efforts was Odalis Perez, who would have given up nearly six more runs in the 14.7 relief innings thrown by Gagne in Perez's starts. Conversely, Gagne appeared in 3 of the 12 games started by Andy Ashby in 2003, and can be accused of allowing nearly one run more than what Ashby would have done on his own in those 3.7 innings—the only instance for any of the Los Angeles starters when Gagne gave up more runs than what the starter would have allowed.

While the Adjusted Runs Prevented totals quite clearly confirm a phenomenal season, examination of the surgeonlike precision with which Gagne performed should leave no doubt of it. Any pitcher called upon to close the door on 55 wins while having to throw only a single pitch with runners on both second and third base at the same time, as was the case with Gagne,

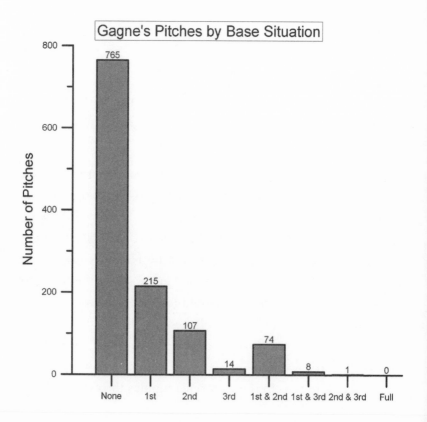

cannot be written off as lucky—especially when one considers the manner in which he was most often used: starting the ninth inning of a save situation.

According to the pitch-by-pitch game logs available through ESPN.com's baseball website, Gagne threw 1,184 pitches, a figure slightly different from the 1,189 pitches credited to him in the season totals by both ESPN.com and the official site of Major League Baseball. While acknowledging this discrepancy, analysis of the individual game logs produce a compilation not only of the number of pitches thrown in a given appearance but also the game situation of each pitch thrown. Gagne not only limited the opposition to a mere 12 runs in 82.3 innings, he found himself in the unenviable position of having two runners in scoring position *once* in nearly 1,200 pitches.

Along with the base situation pitch totals, we can also determine that Gagne's median pitch count was 14, a number made more impressive by his use of the strikeout to retire batters. In needing only 14 pitches to retire an average of just over three batters per appearance, the only way one should suspect a high strikeout rate would be through an equally high ratio of strikes thrown. As suspected, Gagne's ability to throw strikes on 69 percent of his pitches helped quiet opposing bats.

No doubt baseball is a game different from most all others, and this is no more obvious than when one examines the central element of the game: the pitcher-batter confrontation. There are few, if any, instances in all of sport in which the normal manner of competition is that of nine versus one, as it is in baseball.

Examining the game in this manner, one can plainly see that a great deal of baseball is a strictly individual matter. Accordingly, and with little surprise, batting statistics are wholly individual in nature. Yet while some batting numbers are simply a

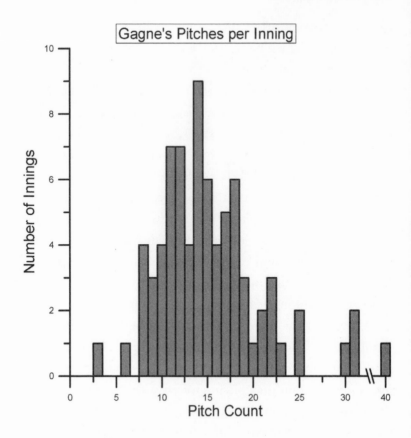

means to account for the numerous possible outcomes that can result from a single plate appearance, others attempt to explain the rate at which certain events occur for an individual batter. All of these statistics, however, are central to the underlying notion that the batter's only true goal is to put himself in position to score by avoiding making an out.

Upon identifying this goal, we can see that the rate at which outs are avoided, otherwise known as on-base percentage (OBP), has proven to be an extremely valuable commodity, though quite clearly not the only commodity worth pursuing. The problem is that while a batsman carrying a 1.000 on-base percentage can be said with certainty to have perfectly avoided making an out at the plate, the figure alone is not enough to guarantee a subsequent run. The reason, quite simply, is that an individual's on-base percentage in no way shows whether or not his teammates have, through their own plate appearances, forced him into making an out on the basepaths, left him on base at the end of an inning, or enabled him to cross home plate safely with a run.

Thus pitching statistics should be more than simply an account of the opposition's batting statistics. Whereas an individual batter's control is vastly limited once he no longer is the individual being pitched to, the man on the mound is keyed into every at-bat of the game. To better illustrate this point, let us examine two separate one-inning situations.

INNING ONE
Batter A: base on balls
Batter B: ground out, 6-4-3 double play
Batter C: single
Batter D: flyout

INNING TWO
Batter A: strikeout
Batter B: strikeout
Batter C: safe on fielder's error
Batter D: flyout

In the above examples it is evident that using the batter's metric of on-base percentage, the innings were quite different. In Inning One the offense produced a .500 OBP, whereas Inning Two's performance produced a .000 OBP. While no manager, executive, or devoted fan would turn his nose up at the prospect of his team maintaining a .500 OBP, this figure alone is clearly not enough to guarantee runs.

From the pitcher's point of view, however, both of the above innings were completed in an equally efficient manner. In both instances, three outs were produced and the pitcher faced only four batters. The question is, how much credit does the pitcher deserve for the above results? For unlike the case of the batter, the pitcher is not alone in his dealings. Eight other players play an important role in helping the pitcher achieve the team's stated goal: preventing runs.

Tom Tippett, in a July 2003 article for SABR, produced research in which he suggested that pitchers can in fact have an effect on the batting average of balls put into play. The conclusion to be drawn from Tippett's study is that the pitcher's abilities have a great deal of impact on the eventual result of individual plate appearances. Whether that's because an individual pitcher increases the likelihood of a strikeout, or lessens the chances of a walk or home run, or affects the overall probability that any ball put in play will result in an out, a pitcher impacts individual plate appearances and should be credited or discredited accordingly.

While a batter's ultimate goal is easily broken down into the concept of avoiding outs, a pitcher is charged with the responsibility of preventing runs by creating outs in any number of ways. The higher the ratio of outs to batters faced, the better a pitcher figures to be in accomplishing his task.

For pitchers, the concept of perfection within the game of baseball has a rather strict definition. "Perfect" games are reserved only for those select few who can retire every batter faced throughout the course of a single ball game—twenty-seven up, twenty-seven down. Those able to achieve perfection at the most opportune of times find with it immortality as a rather pleasant by-product (see Larson, Don).

In a game that presents each at bat with a limitless array of possibilities, the easiest way a pitcher can guarantee the absolute prevention of opposition runs is in fact to be "perfect." Retiring every batter faced will, without fail, produce a shutout. The reason for this is quite simple: if every batter faced makes an out, there is no possible scenario in which a run can be scored. As such, it should follow that we might be able to gain a reasonable understanding about the level of a pitcher's performance by simply determining how close a given pitcher comes to achieving "perfection" over a period of time.

In 40 of his 77 appearances during 2003, Gagne faced only the minimum number of batters for the amount of innings he pitched (for example, two innings, six batters). Ignoring for a moment those games in which he entered in mid-inning, Gagne assured his team of the complete prevention of runs in what appears to be an amazingly high frequency of just over half his appearances.

Each plate appearance needn't result directly in an out in order for perfect run prevention to be attained; there simply needs to be an *average* of exactly three batters faced per inning pitched. Thus a pitcher might allow as many as 18 hits over nine innings while still maintaining a perfect ratio—provided two base hits open each inning while the third batter hits into a triple play.

In considering the ratio of batters faced to innings pitched, note the similarities with Craig Wright's ground-breaking concept of Batters Faced per Start (BFS). Whereas BFS can be used to evaluate pitcher workload, with an eye toward forecasting performance drop-offs and even injuries, the use of batters faced to innings pitched can be seen as a form of dominance ratio in charting starters and relievers alike.

What such a dominance ratio does not do, however, is tell us how close a pitcher's performance is to "perfect" in a way that is easily comparable to other pitchers. In again considering

Gagne's 2003 season, we can readily see that in 82.3 innings he faced 306 batters. Had Gagne faced only the minimum, he would have needed to face only 247 batters. Thus he was 59 batters over the "perfect" value. Those extra 59 batters account for roughly 24 percent more than had Gagne pitched "perfectly" throughout the 2003 season. Nominalizing this value with 100 percent as a perfect score, Gagne's performance achieved approximately 76 percent of total "perfection" in 2003.

This freestanding 76 percent figure has little value outside a well-stated context, but looking at data for the past ten major league seasons provides a suitable starting point. Between the first pitch of 1994 and the final out of the 2003 season, 22,708 regular season games were played at the major league level. In those games, over 1.76 million plate appearances occurred in exactly 405,394 innings pitched.

By calculating the corresponding dominance ratio, and nominalizing it to the same scale as Gagne's figure of 76 percent in 2003, we can see that the corresponding percentage for all major league pitchers over the past ten seasons is approximately 55 percent. Further, in looking at the individual totals for each of the ten seasons, the range can be easily identified as between 56.24 percent (in 2002) and 53.34 percent (in 2000).

We can infer from these figures that the average major league game over the past ten seasons has been pitched at a level only slightly more than halfway to the level of "perfection." This seems intuitively appropriate when one considers that pitching a perfect game is among the most difficult accomplishments in the game.

Further investigation shows the usefulness of this figure in comparing different pitchers. By keeping the total innings pitched at a constant 200, one can see that continually adding

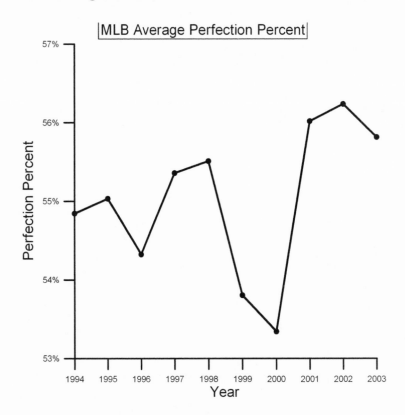

batters faced in increments of 10 produces a linear relationship with regard to the corresponding percentage.

With that we introduce the "Perfection Percentage." The equation of *Perfection Percentage = 2 − 1/3 (BF/IP)* allows us to quickly and rather easily determine exactly how close to perfect a pitcher has performed over a given period of time.

Perfection Percentage is bound by a maximum value of 100 percent at one end of the spectrum, while the other end of the scale is a dreaded "divide by zero." In the case of all pitchers able to record at least one out, a negative value becomes possible once the dominance ratio of BF to IP exceeds 6 to 1.

Perfection Percentage does not account, nor make adjustments, for the help or harm done by fielders, such as double

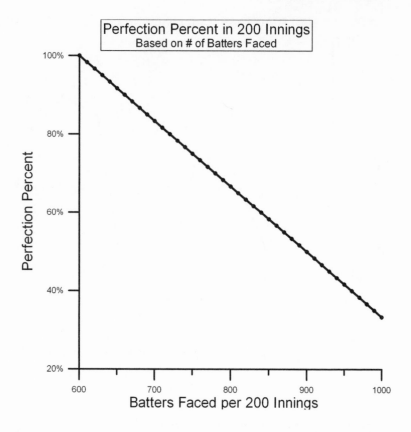

plays or errors. What it quite clearly does measure, however, is the efficiency with which pitchers create outs. Efficiency breeds innings with low pitch counts and can lead to complete games if done consistently. While not as much a concern for relievers, efficiency can be seen in "quick work."

But you may ask, How is Perfection Percentage better than a simple measure such as Earned Run Average? In order to answer this, we must first consider the idea presented in *The Hidden Game of Baseball*, a seminal sabermetric work by John Thorn and Pete Palmer. That book presents a table with which a person can easily look up the probable number of runs that would be scored for a given bases and outs scenario.

The probabilities are based on years of game data, a sample size far greater than a single individual's total of innings pitched for a season. Thus, due to the small sample size that is inherent in ERA, a somewhat unmeasurable amount of luck can adversely or beneficially impact the final measure. Further, not all runs are designated as being earned, though often this determination is somewhat arbitrarily left to the official scorekeeper to decide.

In the case of Perfection Percentage, runs, both earned and otherwise, are left to the probability calculations. Instead we focus on the understanding that fewer batters faced per inning pitched will decrease the probability of runs being scored.

Dealing only in batters faced and innings pitched means that walks, hits, errors, and hit batsmen all essentially count the same. Thus in comparison to the nine-walk, one-beanball, no-hit performance of the Marlin's A. J. Burnett on May 12, 2001, Kerry Wood's 1998 performance against Houston grades out far better by a margin of 92.59 percent versus 62.96 percent. This result runs counter to the obvious fact that Burnett's performance was well celebrated for being of the no-hit variety. While one mustn't look beyond Andy Hawkins to realize that even all no-hitters are not created equally, there is another reason why Wood's game is considered a possible selection for the title of "Greatest Game Ever Pitched" while Burnett's is not: Wood's twenty strikeouts.

In highlighting another interesting aspect of Perfection Percentage, we note that Kerry Wood's record-setting outing would have been unchanged in the eyes of Perfection Percentage had he struck out two, ten, or even twenty-seven batters. (Only one man would have reached first base in any event.) Perfection Percentage can be an incredibly useful tool, but it is by no means the Swiss Army knife of baseball statistics.

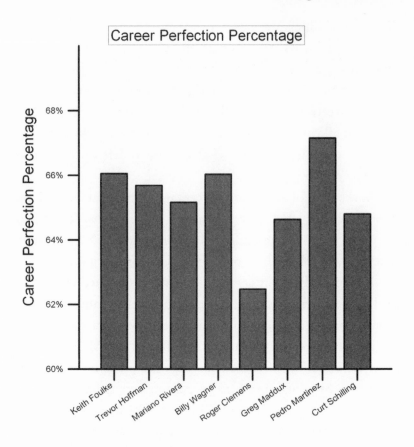

Examining a handful of current major league pitchers shows that rankings based solely on Perfection Percentage appear to be relatively in line with the common consensus of who the leading pitchers in the game currently are. The one obvious distinction is that today's closers exhibit career marks that as a whole are better than even those of the top tier of starting pitchers—which seems logical considering the differences between the two roles. Closers are expected to work efficiently for little more than a single inning at a time, and if they do not perform to a specified level, they will not be long for the job. And, in many cases with closers, a big inning has the potential to end prematurely with either a blown save and a loss, or a change of

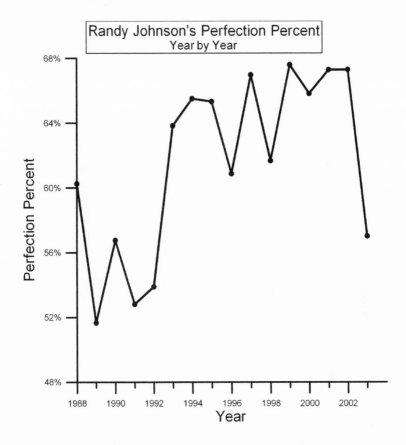

pitcher. In both instances, a closer's batters-faced totals would appear less than those of a premier starting pitcher asked to pitch out of a mid-game jam.

Randy Johnson did not truly become a Cy Young–caliber pitcher until well into his career, something that can be seen clearly in the season-by-season chart of his career's Perfection Percentages. Before 1993 Johnson led the league in walks three consecutive years, averaging more than six walks per game in both 1991 and 1992. In 1993, however, he curtailed his control problems and went on to a career Perfection Percentage of 65.59 percent over the next ten seasons, doing so with a great deal of consistency helped by his 12.03 strikeouts per nine innings.

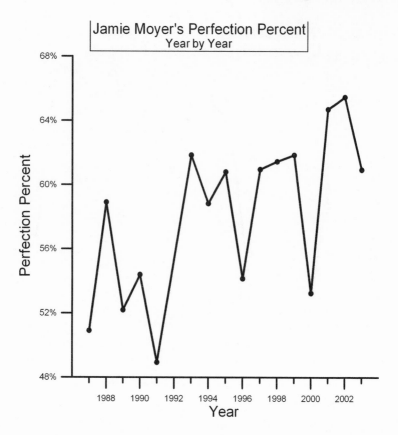

Meanwhile Jamie Moyer has been appropriately credited in the later stages of his career with a masterful ability to limit the batting average of balls in play by his opponents. Corresponding to this newfound ability, Moyer's Perfection Percentage has changed rather dramatically over the past several seasons.

Fans of the reliever Arthur Rhodes may be quick to point out that the left-hander's 2002 Perfection Percentage figure of 77.03 was actually higher than that of Gagne's—76.11 in 2003. This brings forward the idea of combining Perfection Percentage with strikeout rates for a more complete overall evaluation, because strikeout rates are important in understanding the repeatability of a pitcher's level of dominance.

Take, for example, the following two pitchers:

Pitcher A: 100 IP, 300 BF, 50 K
Pitcher B: 100 IP, 300 BF, 200 K

Strikeouts produce a noticeably intuitive difference between two otherwise equal pitchers, both of whom produced a perfect efficiency in creating outs. Pitcher B appears more dominant over-all, and more likely to maintain such a level of perfect dominance. For even though pitchers have a degree of control over the batting average of balls put into play, outs produced in this manner are not nearly as guaranteed as a strikeout. Thus Pitcher A leaves him-self more open to the possibility of baserunners being created by bad hops eating up infielders, and other misadventures. In two pitchers of nearly equal Perfection Percentage, as is the case with Gagne and Rhodes, the pitcher with a higher strikeout rate should have a better chance of repeating an established level of Perfection Percentage.

Taking nothing away Rhodes in a season when he exceeded the out-creation efficiency of the average of his peers by 22 per-cent, his well-above-average strikeout rate of 10.46 per nine in-nings still falls shy of Gagne's 14.98 strikeouts per nine innings in 2003. Based on these figures, Gagne could be given a slight edge in being able to repeat his results.

Having already discussed Gagne's median pitch count of 14, we can now examine his efficiency based on the number of pitches thrown in each appearance. Noting the chart, it should come as no shock that when throwing fewer than the median number of pitches, Gagne's already sky-high Perfection Per-centage begins to take orbit. In 29.3 innings over 31 appear-ances in which Gagne threw 13 pitches or less, his overall Perfection Percentage was a staggering 88.51. In 11 appear-ances when throwing between 8 and 10 pitches, he needed a total of a mere 99 pitches to record 11 innings against 34 batters, representing a Perfection Percentage of 96.97 and an average of 2.91 pitches per batter faced.

When stretched beyond the 14-pitch-count median, Gagne's Perfection Percentage drops to 68.66—still 13 percent above the league average pitcher. In those 37 appearances and 44.7 innings pitched, Gagne threw 737 pitches to 176 batters, an average of 4.19 pitches per batter faced.

It may seem that the more pitches per batter faced Gagne threw, the greater the impact on his Perfection Percentage. But there is not a large enough sample from this data to draw such a conclusion. Further investigation of such a phenomenon, however, could prove to be immensely valuable in breaking down the numerous pitching philosophies about approaches to setting up hitters. Can an individual pitch truly be said to have been perfect, or merely appropriate?

Either way, the most notable impact of Gagne's remarkable relationship between pitches per batter faced and Perfection Percentage is the understanding that when he was "on," opposing batters would have been no less effective swinging a nine-iron wildly around the batter's box. More than any other aspect of his game log, that is the key piece of evidence in any ill-advised arbitration hearing between the pitcher and his employer: he was far too quick to finish innings. Gagne faced only 3 batters in one-inning appearances an amazing 34 times in 77 appearances. By the time fans could write "G-A-G-N-E" on their scorecards, the game was already over.

1-2-3-4, What the Heck Are We Counting For?

In an era when pitchers are not asked to complete games, why then is the most popular emerging statistic the pitch count?

Pitch count is not even a statistic; it is the simplest of counting metrics. Each pitch thrown is marked and noted, a tally kept or a button on a hand-counter clicked. Curveball for a strike? Click. Slider, down and away. Click. Few metrics are simpler or more easily understood.

But the measure of usefulness of any statistic is this: what does it tell us? Pitch count tells us nothing more than the number of pitches thrown by a particular pitcher. In context it can suggest the relative efficiency of a starter. The stat, however, has been used incorrectly. It is not a good measure for what we are trying to accomplish—preventing pitcher fatigue. Common sense tells us that throwing 140 pitches is not a good idea, but there is a world of difference between Randy Johnson throwing 140 pitches over a complete game and Kerry Wood throwing 140 in the summer heat of Wrigley Field. There is also a world of difference between a pitcher who throws 100 pitches over 5.3 innings and a Roy Halladay complete game, 10-inning start . . . that is completed on just 99 pitches.

Supporters of the pitch count disagree on the point at which the pitcher is being damaged. Most agree that 100 is the level when a manager must begin to be concerned; others insist that small differences at this level are insignificant for a single start. Most pitchers have the ability to throw well beyond 100 pitches without serious damage.

A starting pitcher in the Slugging Era (1994–2003) averages about 105 pitches per start and about 6.3 innings per outing. Per inning, this amounts to about 17 pitches. In Halladay's amazing 10-inning, 99-pitch game, he averaged seven pitches less per inning. In an era when old-timers say that pitchers don't complete games anymore due to pitch counts, Halladay points us to the solution to this perceived problem.

It was just a few decades ago that Sandy Koufax went through the 1966 season—his last, pitched with a terminally damaged elbow—and completed twenty-seven games. In 2003 Roy Halladay, Mark Mulder, and Bartolo Colon tied for the major league lead with only nine complete games. Was Koufax a superman who could do three times the work of today's best pitchers, or do we look back on that era less objectively than we do the current one? Koufax's perfect game took him only 107 pitches.

Does the difference lie with the pitchers or the hitters? Most observers will point to the pitchers. Jim Palmer, himself once a workhorse and ace of the Orioles, definitely thinks so. Palmer thinks pitch counts are "terrible. I was never on a pitch count. Kids today play Nintendo or surf the Internet. They aren't out playing in sandlots and learning how to throw a baseball." Palmer, like many, pines for the days of gas for a quarter, two bucks for a bleacher seat, and sandlot baseball. It's a different time, Jim, and baseball is as affected by outside influences as anything else in America. The death of sandlots has less to do with baseball than with a culture of fear and litigation.

If strength and stamina are the difference in pitchers between eras, we could expect that pitchers of the past would not only throw more but throw harder. This is clearly not the case. Some sources say that seventeen pitchers threw at least one pitch of 100 miles per hour during the 2003 season. Yes, there were fewer complete games, but one of the root causes is not stamina but inefficiency.

Watching ESPN Classic can be a lesson. Sluggers of past eras often look about as bulky as today's middle infielder. The lean strength of DiMaggio or Mays doesn't compare to the Herculean physiques of even today's bench players. Modern training techniques, occasionally combined with performance enhancers, have made the home run an omnipresent threat to the modern pitcher. Pitchers now have to respect almost every hitter.

Facing the Cardinals in the 1985 World Series, Tom Niedenfuer looked in at Ozzie Smith. Smith, one of the all-time great fielders in the game's history, stood five feet eleven inches and would be described generously as skinny. (His listing of 150 pounds may be one of the few accurate weights in all baseball history.) Made famous by Jack Buck's "Go crazy, folks!" call on the radio, Smith's home run is remembered as much for the sheer unexpectedness of it as for the result. In that 1985 season, Smith hit only 6 homers—his career high. He hit only 28 over his career.

There are few Ozzie Smiths in today's game. While Ryne Sandberg and Joe Morgan are remembered among the greatest of second basemen, both were odd in that they possessed power in addition to the more normal skills set for a middle infielder in their respective eras. Instead, baseball today is populated with the likes of Brett Boone and Alex Rodriguez, players with fifty-home-run potential and tape-measure power. Rodriguez will soon set the career record for home runs as a shortstop. He will be twenty-eight when he passes Cal Ripken's record in just under half the number of at bats.

Beyond efficiency, there is effort. In the modern game of baseball there are no easy outs, no players for whom a pitcher can throw a ball down the fat part of the plate and know with near certainty that the ball will stay in the park. Pitchers who racked up higher pitch counts, like Bob Feller, often "took batters off," throwing one or two hittable pitches to the bottom of the order, knowing they would likely hit easy grounders rather than towering bombs. Pitchers would dare players to hit the ball, taking something off the pitch and leaving the breaking stuff in their pockets.

If modern pitchers are to go deeper into games, they must become more efficient in both their mechanics and their pitch counts. Halladay proves that it's possible, if difficult, since the cost of error is statistically higher in the Slugging Era. Is it possible, even probable, that other pitchers can follow this example? Of course, but a better question is, do they need to? Pitchers have one job on the mound. It is not to win games, save games, throw strikes, or throw hard—though if asked, this would be the answer many would give. It is simpler. A pitcher is asked to prevent runs.

Run prevention is a much more difficult task to perform and to measure. It is perhaps best expressed by a converse of the measure for hitters: runs created. For pitchers, "runs saved" is based on a complex formula that is roughly the opposite of runs created. But while runs saved is a good measure, it doesn't account for external factors or allow for easy comparison between players on other teams or from different eras.

Again, we look to researcher Lee Sinins. The creator of an electronic baseball encyclopedia, Sinins based his work on the two interrelated measures of runs created and runs saved. "Saving runs is the pitcher's job," says Sinins. "Whether a team wins or loses a game is determined by the combination of the team's offensive and defensive components. The offense, which is 50 percent of the equation, consists completely of other people's contributions. The defensive component also consists of the relievers and the fielding.

"So whether a team wins or loses a game is determined more by the combined efforts of everyone else than it is by a starting pitcher. Add in the near random factor that whether or not the pitcher even gets a 'win' or 'loss' is determined by the luck of the draw on when his teammates, or the other lineup, gets credit for that stupid, abandoned stat of Game Winning RBI."

For purposes of comparison, Sinins does not leave the statistics in their simplest form but adjusts them compared to league average. With this refinement, Runs Created Against Average (RCAA) and Runs Saved Against Average (RSAA) serve as a very accurate measure of a pitcher's ability.

Asked why he uses the average for comparison, Sinins explains, "Comparing a player to a made-up awful one asks the wrong question. I'm not interested in trying to estimate how much better a player is than a hypothetical terrible one. I'm interested in trying to determine whether a player helps his team win or lose games, and by how much he does it. Whether a player helps your team win or lose—I'll bet that's what you're really interested in too."

Sinins illustrates his approach with examples. "League average isn't just some abstract concept, rather it is the level that separates whether a player helps his team win or lose games. If, for example, the league averages 4.81 runs per team per game, like the 2002 American League, it means that a team has to score more than 4.81 runs to win the average game. So a player who has created 4.81 runs per 27 outs is performing right at average level, not pushing his team more toward winning or losing, while a 4.82+ player moves his team more toward winning and below 4.81 moves them more toward losing."

I asked Sinins if a player worth zero RCAA or RSAA was good or bad. He answered, "That player isn't doing nothing. He merely balanced positives and negatives, resulting in no net gain or loss to the team. He certainly did better than a player with a double-digit negative RCAA/RSAA, and should be seen as a better player. He should be accepted for what he is—average. That's what the zero shows. To say it shows nothingness is a misinterpretation of what systems based on an average baseline try to measure."

Despite the clear value of Sinins's RSAA, there is considerable debate in the baseball analysis community about the baseline against which players should be judged. For many, including Sinins, judging players against an average is considered best. Others believe that measuring players against a concept known as "replacement value" offers a truer comparison. In *Baseball Prospectus 2001*, Keith Woolner wrote, "If value in baseball is driven by maximizing wins (or, almost equivalently, maximizing the likelihood of reaching the postseason and then winning the World Series), this freely available resource [replacement-level players] is the zero point in value. Teams win more often than others only if they field better talent than what is freely available." The truth of this statement is readily apparent when one looks at the Yankees and the Tigers circa 2003, but it goes beyond the tired small-market arguments.

Woolner goes on to discuss how he arrives at replacement level mathematically and graphically, but finally he comes to an easily stated conclusion: "Replacement level is the expected level of performance a major league team will receive from one or more of the best available players who substitute for a suddenly unavailable starting player at the same position, and who can be obtained with minimal expenditure of team resources." What Woolner has done, then, is to change the baseline for comparison from a set of all players to a point below the expected point of major league value. Woolner's statistic Value Over Replacement Player (VORP) uses this calculated baseline to determine values, in runs, for every player and pitcher.

Both methods are valid. Where one may have an advantage over the other is in context. When Derek Jeter dislocated his shoulder, comparing Erick Almonte (his replacement during the injury) to the average told very little, but looking at Jeter's VORP could provide an insight into what the Yankees could expect to lose during Jeter's time on the shelf. In other situations, like season-long comparisons of players, especially pitchers, an average-based metric gives a clear view toward the ranking of pitchers.

Were this a book on statistics alone, I would discuss innovations such as Support Neutral pitching statistics, another Baseball Prospectus property that removes run support from pitching statistics, and Reliever Run Evaluations, a better tool for monitoring the success or failure of relievers than is available elsewhere. Both metrics are the brainchildren of Michael Wolverton, and I encourage everyone to look at his work at baseballprospectus.com.

Another method of evaluating pitchers that must be mentioned, at least in passing, is Bill James's Win Shares method. Win Shares is a complex series of calculations that seeks to divide a team's wins proportionally between a team's players. The more valuable a player, the more Win Shares that player is granted. James's past work in the field has been groundbreaking, but Win Shares has faced resistance due to its inscrutably difficult formula and James's insistence that it has no value except after the fact. James's focus on history, in works such as *The Politics of Glory* and *The New Historical Abstract*, help explain why he would employ a tool so powerful but only in hindsight.

I do not possess the level of mathematical skills to pass judgment on Win Shares as a method for assessing pitchers. James obviously created a valuable tool for what he sought to do— compare players across generations. Whether that tool should be used in anything other than that context remains to be seen.

Another James invention that holds more promise in the short term is Game Scores. First published in James's 1987 *Abstract* as a "garbage stat," Game Scores seeks to give a value to a pitcher's start. James calculated Game Scores as starting with 50 points. The pitcher is then given one additional point for each batter retired, two points for each inning compiled after the fourth, and one point for every strikeout. Points are also subtracted: two for each hit allowed, four for each earned run, two for each unearned run, and one point for each walk.

Using this method gives us a "quick and dirty" way of assessing a pitcher's performance, which is easier to use than a pitcher's line in a box score. It also encapsulates much more information than the flawed metric of "quality start," baseball's measure that awards a quality start after a pitcher goes six or more innings and gives up three earned runs or less. Clearly a pitcher could have a number of quality starts and never sniff a win. For once Joe Morgan has it right when he says the quality start is "the invention of some sportswriter that means nothing." Other statistics along this line purport to be more useful and informative, notably Ron Shandler's "Pure Quality Start," but the Game Score hits a sweet spot between information and complexity.

James, in his original essay, said Game Score was nothing but junk—fun, but not something he felt particularly strong about at the time. Still, through the years since and the use of his Game Score by such writers as Rob Neyer (once James's research assistant), it has become a statistic listed even at ESPN. There is, however, a taint on Game Score since its creator once called it junk. As with any metric, it can be tweaked; and Fox Sports writer Dayn Perry took up the cause, again at Baseball Prospectus.

Perry altered the James Game Score slightly, factoring in considerations that since 1987 have been more widely accepted as important. Again starting with a base of 50 points, Perry's "Game Score 2.0" adds one point for each batter retired, two points for each inning completed after the fifth, and two points for each strikeout. It subtracts two points for each hit allowed, five points for each run allowed (earned or not, with a caveat that the run must not be a home run), four points for each unintentional walk allowed, and seven points for each home run. Perry's formula rewards controlled, efficient pitchers who limit the long ball in a slugging era.

While Perry's version is more sabermetrically informed, James's version remains valid. Since a great score in James's version hovers between 90 and 100, it is slightly easier to read. Like other pitching statistics, it is only in the broadest view where information lies. The quest for the "one true stat" has ruined many smaller, informative statistics that in some cases give us specific information that is hidden in calculated statistics. That's not to say that one approach or the other is right. It is, in the words of Dayn Perry, a "beer or tacos" question—the correct answer is, "Both, you fool!"

Pitcher Abuse Points

The first complete sabermetric attempt at measuring the workload of pitchers was done by Dr. Rany Jazayerli, a writer for Baseball Prospectus. Working from a discussion of workload in *A Diamond Appraised* by Craig Wright and the seemingly omnipresent Tom House, Jazayerli took better statistics and created a tool. His intuitive attempt at measuring workload was based on the concept that damage is cumulative. Setting a threshold at the accepted but unscientific hundred-pitch level, Jazayerli discovered that each successive pitch after one hundred caused a stress level that could best be described as a downward spiral.

NAME	TEA	L	GS	IP	IP/GS	NP	AVGNP	MAXNP	PAP	AVGPAP	STRESS
2 Vazquez_Javier	MON	N	34	230.7	6.8	3719	109.4	136	268015	7883	72
1 Wood_Kerry	CHN	N	32	211	6.6	3516	109.9	141	254622	7957	72
5 Hernandez_Livan	MON	N	33	233.3	7.1	3573	108.3	138	230350	6980	64
3 Prior_Mark	CHN	N	30	211.3	7	3397	113.2	133	223611	7454	66
4 Redman_Mark	FLO	N	29	190.7	6.6	3159	108.9	140	207590	7158	66
9 Williams_Woody	SLN	N	33	220	6.7	3624	109.8	132	131785	3993	36
7 Leiter_Al	NYN	N	30	180.7	6	3235	107.8	136	129839	4328	40
11 Ortiz_Russ	ATL	N	34	212.3	6.2	3558	104.6	131	124739	3669	35
10 Schmidt_Jason	SFN	N	29	207.7	7.2	3085	106.4	127	108566	3744	35
16 Pineiro_Joel	SEA	A	32	211.7	6.6	3474	108.6	129	102408	3200	29
17 Zambrano_Carlos	CHN	N	32	214	6.7	3400	106.3	129	100157	3130	29
21 Pettitte_Andy	NYA	A	33	208.3	6.3	3380	102.4	126	88919	2695	26
25 Colon_Bartolo	CHA	A	34	242	7.1	3519	103.5	131	84591	2488	24
15 Gonzalez_Jeremi	TBA	A	25	156.3	6.3	2709	108.4	125	84256	3370	31
24 Clemens_Roger	NYA	A	33	211.7	6.4	3447	104.5	133	82376	2496	24
19 Zambrano_Victor	TBA	A	28	178.7	6.4	2970	106.1	126	80472	2874	27
22 Martinez_Pedro	BOS	A	29	186.7	6.4	2837	97.8	128	77799	2683	27
12 Suppan_Jeff	PIT	N	21	141	6.7	2166	103.1	132	75214	3582	35
13 Ponson_Sidney	BAL	A	21	148	7	2118	100.9	134	73982	3523	35
26 Johnson_Jason	BAL	A	32	189.7	5.9	3151	98.5	127	73361	2293	23
20 Escobar_Kelvim	TOR	A	26	163	6.3	2640	101.5	131	72220	2778	27
28 Thomson_John	TEX	A	35	217	6.2	3326	95	134	72012	2057	22
23 Lopez_Rodrigo	BAL	A	26	147	5.7	2483	95.5	126	66582	2561	27
30 Wolf_Randy	PHI	N	33	200	6.1	3252	98.5	131	63983	1939	20
38 Zito_Barry	OAK	A	35	231.7	6.6	3730	106.6	122	58018	1658	16
36 Sheets_Ben	MIL	N	34	220.7	6.5	3352	98.6	127	57367	1687	17
33 Padilla_Vicente	PHI	N	32	208.7	6.5	3168	99	129	54913	1716	17
31 Perez_Odalis	LAN	N	30	185.3	6.2	2856	95.2	132	54592	1820	19
35 Wells_Kip	PIT	N	31	197.3	6.4	3192	103	126	52714	1700	17
32 Mussina_Mike	NYA	A	30	209.7	7	3138	104.6	122	52294	1743	17
27 Helling_Rick	BAL	A	24	138.7	5.8	2409	100.4	126	50829	2118	21
45 Hudson_Tim	OAK	A	34	240	7.1	3485	102.5	127	50490	1485	14
37 Sabathia_CC	CLE	A	30	197.7	6.6	3131	104.4	120	50404	1680	16
43 Garcia_Freddy	SEA	A	33	201.3	6.1	3356	101.7	123	50225	1522	15
41 Hampton_Mike	ATL	N	31	190	6.1	2970	95.8	128	49216	1588	17
44 Trachsel_Steve	NYN	N	33	204.7	6.2	3316	100.5	126	49103	1488	15
29 Weaver_Jeff	NYA	A	24	147.7	6.2	2458	102.4	122	48821	2034	20
42 Rogers_Kenny	MIN	A	31	193.3	6.2	3076	99.2	131	48204	1555	16
6 Drese_Ryan	TEX	A	8	37	4.6	668	83.5	136	46656	5832	70
39 Stephenson_Garrett	SLN	N	27	165.3	6.1	2622	97.1	124	43699	1618	17
40 Morris_Matt	SLN	N	27	172.3	6.4	2506	92.8	125	43626	1616	17
51 Millwood_Kevin	PHI	N	35	222	6.3	3474	99.3	118	43190	1234	12
48 Seo_Jae_Weong	NYN	N	31	183.3	5.9	2846	91.8	132	41085	1325	14
55 Halladay_Roy	TOR	A	36	266	7.4	3612	100.3	122	41023	1140	11
34 Schilling_Curt	ARI	N	24	168	7	2450	102.1	126	40945	1706	17
52 Nomo_Hideo	LAN	N	33	218.3	6.6	3260	98.8	123	39962	1211	12
53 Peavy_Jake	SDN	N	32	194.7	6.1	3217	100.5	126	37070	1158	12
8 Davis_Doug	MIL	N	8	52.3	6.5	874	109.3	126	33885	4236	39
46 Beckett_Josh	FLO	N	23	141	6.1	2265	98.5	123	30963	1346	14
49 Hentgen_Pat	BAL	A	21	133.7	6.4	2163	103	117	27360	1303	13
50 Vargas_Claudio	MON	N	20	109.3	5.5	1795	89.8	120	25902	1295	14
18 Condrey_Clay	SDN	N	6	30.3	5.1	554	92.3	126	17576	2929	32
14 Wright_Jamey	KCA	A	4	25.3	6.3	374	93.5	124	13824	3456	37
54 Dreifort_Darren	LAN	N	10	60.3	6	986	98.6	120	11481	1148	12
47 Austin_Jeff	CIN	N	7	28.3	4	544	77.7	121	9386	1341	17

How stress increases at pitch counts over 100.

As you can see from this chart, the stress caused by pitch 141 is significantly greater than that caused by pitch 121. By working out the levels at which pitchers not only lose effectiveness but begin to accumulate significant damage, Jazayerli's system took pitch counts and pitch monitoring beyond a mere counting stat.

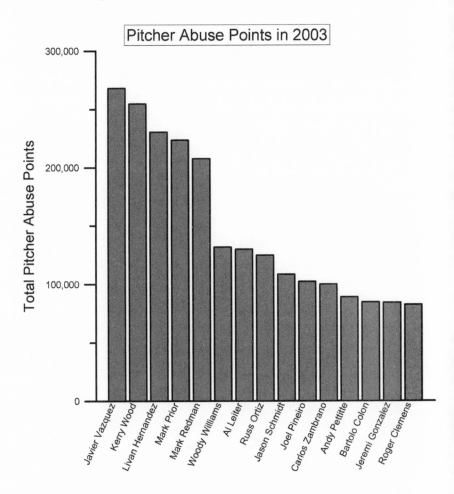

Keith Woolner, one of the world's top sabermetricians, took Jazayerli's system to another level when he added complexity and accuracy to the Pitcher Abuse Points (PAP) system. Woolner's work showed that each additional pitch did not do additive damage but in fact did geometric damage. Oversimplifying Woolner's adjustments to the system, each pitch was taken to the third power (cubed) and then looked at both cumulatively and in three start blocks.

Beyond the complex mathematics, PAP[3] has one important and easily understood result: a pitcher with a high pitch count shows significantly reduced effectiveness over his next starts. This result, backed by the mathematical proofs of Woolner and Jaza-yerli, provides the first incontrovertible evidence that high pitch counts in one start have a significant cost over the pitcher's next outings. Thus a manager must consider if having a pitcher go extra in this start will detract from his effectiveness in the next start.

PAP—that is the Woolner-adjusted PAP[3] version—stands up not only to mathematical but also to real world testing. From the 2003 season, here is an example below.

Clearly, Wood suffered a serious and significant drop-off beyond a certain level, in this case 120 pitches. Somehow this news didn't make it to the Cubs dugout, and like most fatigue condi-

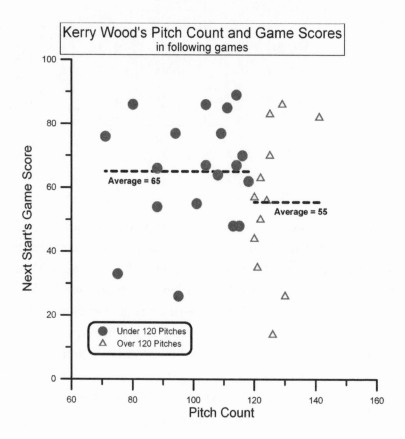

tions, it was the cumulative effect that came home to roost. In game seven of the National League Championship Series, Wood took the mound following three straight playoff outings in which he cleared the 100-pitch mark. By the fifth inning Wood appeared to have nothing left, and his team certainly did not. While Wood took the loss hard, blaming himself, pitching analysts pointed the finger at his manager and coaches for putting him in a situation where he was more likely to fail than succeed.

In 2003 Bill James contested the findings of Jazayerli and Woolner, stating that at its core, it fails to measure workload as it purports to do. His work, to be published after the writing of this book, was generously shared with me, and his conclusions do show a weakness in the system. Other attacks on the system, most famously by a bitter failed rival, Don Malcolm, have not weakened the standing of PAP as the best available tool for measuring workload that becomes abuse.

The weakness James addresses—which may turn out to be a strength of the PAP system—is in assessing pitchers who seemingly buck the system. Some, like C. C. Sabathia or Livan Hernandez, appear to be sponges, soaking up both innings and abuse that would send most pitchers, especially young ones, screaming and running to Dr. Frank Jobe. While no scientific work has been done to determine if the PAP system can determine who can and cannot absorb a seemingly excessive workload, it is intuitive that names that show up year after year at the top of the PAP charts are more likely both to put up big cumulative pitch counts and to break down spectacularly.

Of all the lessons of PAP, this is the most important: a manager and pitching coach must put their pitchers, from their ace starter to their mop-up reliever, in situations where they are best suited to succeed. These pitchers must be mentally and physically prepared, they must have the mental toughness to deal with their particular role, and their physical gifts must be honed by proper practice and physical conditioning.

Velocity Loss

While Pitcher Abuse Points are a tested means of measuring pitcher fatigue and workload, it is far from an easy method. It demands careful explanation, and few people can do exponentiation in their heads. Pitch counts are an easy measure—anyone can count, even to 140. Is there, then, a measure that is as simple and intuitive as pitch count but can approximate the accuracy of PAP?

Preliminary research indicates that there is. Measuring pitch velocity is nothing new. Even before radar guns were available, people attempted to judge pitch speed. The legendary tale of Steve Dalkowski pitching to match the speed of a car racing past him is actually true. When accurately measured, velocity can be used to chart fatigue.

The principle of Velocity Loss (which I refer to as V-loss) is simple: as a pitcher tires, he will lose a percentage of velocity, as measured from his fastball. While it is impossible to measure fatigue without complicated and often invasive testing, it is relatively easy to measure the speed of a fastball. The first task of analyzing V-loss is to establish the level of the fastball. It is important to get multiple readings from a consistent, measured source. Following V-loss requires a simple charting system. Readers of my "Under the Knife" column participated in charting pitches for the project over the 2002–2003 seasons, showing both pitch type and velocity.

Using this example, we can see that the pitcher established his fastball at 94 miles per hour. There were a couple of pitches at 95 in the first inning, when a pitcher is often excited. It would not surprise me, if we went back to the tape, to find that the pitch at 95 was wild. As we follow this chart into the fifth inning, we see fatigue beginning to set in, as his fastball occasionally dips to 92 and 93. In the sixth inning he fails to reach the established level but is not yet at the danger point, which is set at 3 percent below the established level. In this example the danger point is 91. (Fractions are ignored for reasons of simplicity.) By the seventh inning the pitcher is struggling; his pitches alternate between 90 and 92 miles per hour, and we can likely see greater effort on the higher-velocity pitches.

When the manager sends him back out for the eighth inning, something interesting happens. The velocity returns to the established level. As I first began charting this and seeing this pattern

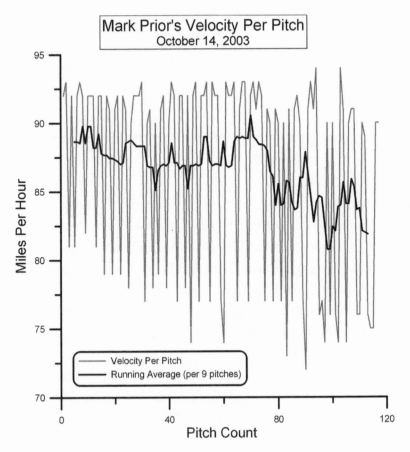

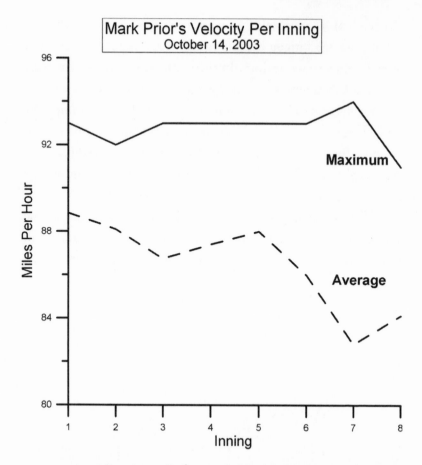

occur repeatedly, I recalled a term from the financial world. Stockbrokers are a morbid lot, and when some poor stocks show a similar pattern—a small comeback after a sharp fall—the term they have for it is "dead cat bounce." In other words, after a fall, almost any item will bounce, at least slightly. While I mean no harm to felines, I've adapted the term to the V-loss work. Pitchers who experience a sudden return to established velocity are called "dead cats."

What explains dead cats? Pitchers have a profound kinesthetic sense. They are often able to discern changes in their pitching motion on a near subconscious level. Pitchers know too when they are losing velocity. Pitchers know when they don't have their best stuff. Pitchers are competitive. It is no surprise that a pitcher, when fatigued and losing velocity in the late innings, will reach back for a bit more and will often find it.

This "reaching back" is usually accomplished by going to a higher-effort motion, altering the mechanics that allow a pitcher to throw with such powerful force in the first place. Most commonly, a pitcher will attempt to exert more force by overrecruiting his shoulder. A powerful contraction in that area seems to make sense and feels productive. It is not. While the higher effort allows the pitcher to return to his established level for a short time, he cannot sustain it very long, often less than an inning. But he is also often altering his mechanics and causing himself physical damage.

Not knowing he has a dead cat on the mound, the manager looks to our example and sees a warrior, a guy who will gut it out, who wants to finish what he started. This manager doesn't realize there is less value in one last inning that leads to a complete game than in the first six innings of his next start. With his first few pitches after his dead-cat resurgence, our example pitcher reaches the breaking point. In our system the breaking point is 5 percent below the established level or, in this case, 89 miles per hour. At this level the pitcher's fatigue has so broken down his normal mechanics and processes that injury often occurs.

You will note that inherent in the system is a pitch count. It is kept and noted, but is of no particular significance. If a pitcher reaches the danger point of velocity at pitch 80, it is of no more or less significance than if it was reached at pitch 120. But one would expect that the pitcher who fatigues earlier will not be able to go deep into games and may find his position as a starter in jeopardy. Other inefficient pitchers might reach both the danger point of velocity *and* a high pitch count in early innings. It is important to the effectiveness and simplicity of the system to focus on velocity, the one measured factor, without allowing context to color the data. While I don't wish to deny the value of context, it should be a judgment made either in the game by the manager or in retrospect by the medical team. Any additional information is simply not part of the system, valuable or not.

V-loss also has an intra-inning component that is difficult to judge. Many organizations have a control mechanism requiring that pitchers be removed after 30 pitches in one inning. Oddly, I have never heard of this control being used in the major leagues. In fact, more than 100 pitchers reached that threshold during the 2003 season, several more than one time and more than a few hitting that count twice during the same game! Luckily the built-in control on this type of abuse is that the pitcher is almost always struggling if he is racking up 30-pitch innings.

V-loss can, however, be profoundly impacted by hitters. In Kerry Wood's 141-pitch outing, he began the ninth inning with just 110 pitches on his arm. Facing the bottom of the lineup, this was a reasonable and defensible move on the part of management. After knocking out the eighth-place hitter in normal fashion, Woody Williams, the Cardinals pitcher, came to the plate. Williams, at best a poor hitter, proceeded to foul off 6 pitches, leading to an 11-pitch out. Then Fernando Vina also fouled off several pitches, adding another 11 to Wood's total before making his own out. A three-up, three-down inning looks good on paper, but in this instance the damage was done.

On a pitch-count basis, the move was defensible, but Wood's velocity was off by the necessary 3 percent in the seventh inning. By the end of the ninth, Wood was down almost 7 percent, but he was still able to hit the mid-90s on certain key pitches. His expression and constant wiping at sweat made both the summer heat and his fatigue as apparent as the ivy on the walls behind him. While it's easy to say that this was apparent—by pitch count, V-loss, or simply looking at the man on the mound—at least two men did not see it the same way. Those two men, the pitching coach and the manager, are the ones that matter.

One criticism of the V-loss system is the inconsistent nature of measurement—in this case, radar guns. This is a problem that can be overcome. While a gun may be inaccurate, recording a speed higher or lower than the true speed, it is usually internally consistent. Results measured over two seasons show that internal consistency not only works in a game but also over the course of a season. The radar gun used by Fox Sports Chicago at U.S. Cellular Field, the home of the White Sox, regularly adds three miles per hour to each pitch. But it *consistently* does this, allowing an observer to use the data accurately even if the measurement itself is slightly off.

V-loss has not only a single-game but also a season-long component, allowing fatigue to be measured over the course of a baseball season or even in some cases over multiple seasons. Sports medicine practitioners have often looked at a loss of velocity as a measure of injury, especially when it occurs suddenly and without external causation. In one case during the 2003 season, a starting pitcher established his fastball at four miles per hour below his previously established levels. As it continued to fade during the game, this velocity loss raised questions about the pitcher's health. After several attempts to get information from the team, I was finally able to discover the truth: the pitcher had showed up for the game with a hangover. When he returned to the mound for his next scheduled start, his velocity established itself at the normal levels.

That case is unusual. More often there is no such excuse, and one must look to the simplest explanation: fatigue. While a pitcher who makes it to the major leagues must have talent, he is not required to have much else. Pitchers can make "the show" with only one good pitch or with abysmal mechanics. They can be overworked at any level. They can have no more idea about the principles of pitching than they know about cold fusion, yet still pitch effectively. As a pitcher fatigues, he tries to maintain a certain level of effectiveness, often without conscious control. The macho culture of sport often celebrates this, but remember that the macho culture of sport eats its own young.

A perfect example of this kind of pitcher is former Brewers prospect Kyle Peterson. A first-round pick, Peterson raced through the minor leagues with excellent results and a pitching motion that made surgeons salivate. Peterson's motion rivaled Darren Dreifort's for awkward violence, including a pause in the midst of the delivery once described as "like a marionette that has briefly had its strings cut."

Leo Mazzone warns against "overextending and overexerting." This is his method of warning his pitchers to "stay within themselves," to maintain their mechanics and resist the temptation to reach back, which might do damage. Mazzone has said, "I'd rather have the guy come out when he's tired. That's why we pay those guys in the bullpen." Mazzone's informed statement shows us that, intuitively, he is monitoring both fatigue and pitcher mechanics while using the modern specialty relief pitcher effectively.

Absent a radar gun, how can the V-loss method work? In an experiment in early 2003, I took three friends to a high school baseball game. I gave them a V-loss chart and asked them to use a slightly different method to record their data. Instead of pitch speed, I asked them to use a ten-point system. 10 would signify the pitcher's absolute best fastball, 9 would signify the established level, while 1 would signify that his arm hangs loosely at his side and he rolls the pitch to the catcher. Each point would indicate a perceived reduction in velocity and measure increasing fatigue.

I sat apart from the subjects, measuring with a calibrated radar gun they could not see. Using the perceived V-loss system, my friends were able to judge the speed of a pitch effectively in a relative manner. In this and other situations at every level, from Little League to the American League Division Series, untrained individuals have often been almost as accurate as the radar gun at judging when a pitcher has reached the danger point (7 on the perceived V-loss scale) and the breaking point (5 on the scale).

Both actual and perceived V-loss can be a valuable tool for measuring pitcher fatigue and determining the proper point for removing a pitcher. Not only does it offer a chance to prevent injuries, it also seeks to maximize the value of any pitcher—starter or reliever—by using him to the point where he ceases to be effective. If V-loss removes some of the guesswork in determining fatigue, we have another tool in the battle to save pitchers.

10

PRACTICAL MATTERS: A TRAINER'S DAY

Dr. William Carroll offers this scenario of the head trainer for a major league baseball team. There are differences among teams based on team policies and the philosophies of the various athletic trainers, but in general the following description accurately depicts the duties of the major league baseball athletic trainer.

(For economy of prose, the male pronoun is used throughout this scenario. While there are no female trainers in the major leagues, there are several in the minor leagues. As the profession continues to attract more and more women, there is a near inevitability to a woman gaining a major league job.)

The trainer rises early each day because he has a lot to do. In order to set things up properly, he must be in the training room at least three hours before the first player is due to arrive. And because his workday is both long and physical, he must be in good shape himself. Because his job is to provide athletic health care to the players, he knows the old saying in athletic training that "the trainer can never be sick." So he must take care of his own health, which means staying in good condition. Since he can never be sure how long his workday will be and what it will bring, he had best get his workout in early. For some this involves running or walking on the treadmill, for others a combination of running or walking and working out with weights.

When he arrives at the training room, he checks phone messages or e-mail and prepares the training room and the players' table for the day's events. In the training room he checks for all the supplies he will need, including tape (several different kinds), prewrap, adherent, Band-Aids, wound cleaning supplies, skin lubricant, talcum powder (rubbed over a taped ankle or foot so that the tape edges will not curl when the player puts on his sock over the taped body part), skin closures or durabond (for lacerations), counterirritants (what used to be called "liniment" but is now in a cream base), second skin and other blister treatments, and the various instruments such as scissors, nail cutters, forceps, tweezers, and cutters for tape removal. The players' table in the clubhouse is stocked with athletic training supplies that players who are not currently being treated may use, such as Band-Aids, skin lubricant, nail cutters, sun-block lotion, and eye black or eye-black strips. He's aware that some of his players will avoid him as much as possible or, potentially worse, become "clubhouse doctors."

Also during this time the head trainer will report players' health status to the manager. Sometimes he will call or send a written report to the club office regarding player health status. If a player will be unable to perform for a period of time, a report must be sent to the league office. This will prompt a discussion with the team doctor or medical director and may involve contracted or outside specialists. The head trainer must also check to ensure that any pieces of emergency equipment (spine board, emergency oxygen, bag valve mask, latex gloves for dealing with bloody wounds, cell phone or walkie-talkies, splints and injury ice bags) are ready for use if needed— including extra batteries and backups for things he might run out of.

The field and dugout must also be prepared for the day's events, a task often made tougher by the layout of some stadiums. This means that towels and water must be ready. Many people do not understand the importance of water for the athlete. If temperature and humidity are high, the athlete will lose a considerable amount of fluid by sweating. But even if temperature and humidity are not above the danger zone, the athlete is still putting forth effort and sweating, so he needs to keep his hydration level up to avoid a heat illness (heat cramps, heat exhaustion, heat stroke).

For proper hydration, the athlete should be encouraged to ingest fluids (water, Gatorade, PowerAde, etc.) at least forty-five minutes before activity. Once activity has begun, players should be encouraged to ingest fluids at least every half-hour, regardless of temperature and humidity. Many times the thirst reflex ("Gee, I'm thirsty—I'd like a cold beverage") is not a good indicator of the amount of fluid the athlete needs, so the trainer needs to monitor his intake. Although Hollywood's negative connotation of "water boy" has been demeaning to professional athletic trainers, the hydration of athletes is extremely important to the athlete's well-being and performance.

Let's assume this is a home game and a night game. This means that the players will be showing up at the stadium for batting practice during the afternoon. There may also be other practice sessions going on in addition to batting practice. Well before this activity is to begin, players will be coming into the training room for treatment and rehabilitation. Intensive treatment or rehab is for players who are injured to the extent that they most likely will not be able to play. These players will arrive first in the training room because their treatment will take longest. The head trainer may check with the team physician regarding his most recent examination of the player and treatment suggestions.

Before treatment, the head trainer will have reviewed the player's medical file, will know what medications he is taking and how often, and will review his notes from the last treatment session with the athlete so that he can evaluate progress. Since most major league training rooms contain state-of-the-art treatment modalities (therapeutic ultrasound, electrical stimulation, diathermy, traction, whirlpools, etc.) and rehab equipment (weight machines, free weights, resistance tubing or bands, hand exercisers, medicine balls, Swiss balls, and even isokinetic equipment), a player's treatment and rehab in most cases can be done on site without referral to an outside facility.

Once the trainer completes the intensive rehab sessions, he moves on to players with less severe injuries that will not prevent them from playing, and players needing or wanting preventive care. These treatments may consist of taping an ankle or wrist, checking a knee brace, checking the healing status of a minor wound, or supervising stretching or massage to a particular body part before the player goes onto the field.

Therapeutic massage still plays a major role in the care and prevention of athletic injuries. Unlike the early baseball trainers who used massage for every injury ("rub some dirt on it!"), today's professional athletic trainers use massage scientifically to accomplish such things as breaking up adhesions from an old injury; minimizing swelling (and therefore minimizing loss of range of motion) from a recent injury; raising the temperature of a particular muscle of muscle group, thereby making it more flexible; and relaxing muscles that may be experiencing spasm or tightness. It is not uncommon for every pitcher on the roster to receive some degree of massage to his throwing shoulder and back (because of the importance of the back muscles for core stabilization during pitching) before going onto the field.

Pitchers have a fairly intricate routine based on when they last pitched and when they will pitch again. Unfortunately, most aren't working under a scientific program. Some pitchers throw every day. Some do not throw at all the day after pitching in a game. Some pitchers do "long toss" drills the day after a starting assignment. These routines are designed to allow the muscles, tendons, and ligaments involved in the throwing motion to rest or heal, and then slowly build them (usually over a four-day period) to a point where the pitcher is able to perform at his best when his turn in the starting rotation comes up again.

For relief pitchers the scenario is different, because they never know when their services will be needed. Long- and middle-relief pitchers follow a routine similar to starting pitchers; short relievers must be ready for action at any time and therefore do not have the luxury of planned rest.

When all the players are on the field for batting or fielding practice, the assistant trainer usually monitors the players on the field in case of injury while the head trainer busies himself with administrative duties. Some of these duties may include making notations in the medical charts of players who have been treated; checking with rehab coordinators at the extended spring-training site for progress reports on players assigned there for rehab; checking with the various minor league trainers within the organization for status reports on injured players with those teams; filing insurance reports; and ordering or replenishing supplies for the treatment area or the players' table.

When the field practice session ends, some players will return to the training room for further treatment. Pitchers will be iced and stretched. Injuries that appear to be responding slowly to treatment may be referred to the team physician for reevaluation. Once all this has been accomplished, the day's second session of intensive rehab begins.

When these duties are completed, it is time to start setting up for the game. Although certain tasks may be delegated to the assistant trainer or to interns, the ultimate responsibility for seeing that things are done right resides with the head trainer. As other players begin arriving for the game, treatments are repeated to get players ready to go on the field. Usually the head trainer spends most of this time with the pitcher scheduled to start the game this night. He massages and stretches the throwing arm, shoulder, and back.

It is now about one hour till game time. Like many others, this has been a very busy day for the trainer, who hasn't had time to break for food since breakfast early this morning. Many trainers keep a liquid supplement such as Nutriment or yogurt smoothies in the refrigerator for times when they simply cannot get away for a more substantial meal. Other times a Snickers really does satisfy—or at least fights off the pangs of hunger.

Approaching game time, the head trainer rechecks his field equipment, puts on his game attire, and takes his place in the dugout. Contrary to what most spectators think, the head trainer does not just watch the game. He has a very specific way of observing his players during the game. He watches the pitchers for any indication of changes in their pitching mechanics that might indicate an injury. He watches players diving to make a catch in the outfield or sliding into a base, since these are elevated risk situations for injuries. Base running can also be dangerous, as evidenced by the injuries suffered by Mark Prior and Marcus Giles in 2003 when they violently collided during a routine play between first and second. Both were fortunate to avoid serious injury, and likely caused at least one grey hair for their trainers.

The head trainer always watches the batter closely. With the vast majority of pitchers in the major leagues throwing at velocities greater than ninety miles per hour, the amount of time it takes the ball to travel from the pitcher's hand to the hitting zone allows the batter very little time to react to a ball heading for his body. Millions of people watched on television in 1994 as Kirby Puckett of the Minnesota Twins was struck in the helmet by a fastball. It seemed as if trainer Dick Martin was at the plate alertly rendering aid almost before Puckett hit the ground. Fortunately Puckett was not in danger of becoming the first player since Roy Chapman to be killed by a pitch, but the incident emphasized the actions of a truly professional athletic trainer who knew what aspect of the game produced the greatest risk of injury. Martin kept his eyes on the player and then reacted rapidly and calmly to prevent risk of further injury.

Yogi Berra has been credited with the saying, "The game isn't over till it's over"—but then again, he also says, "I didn't say all those things I said." For the professional baseball athletic trainer, the end of the game certainly is hardly the end of his workday. Any injury occurring during the game is treated, and all pitchers who have had action during the game are iced and stretched. Supplies and equipment from the dugout are moved back into the training room for the night. Supplies used during the game are replenished, and notations are made in the medical records of any players treated during or after the game. The head trainer confers with the team physician about any players whom the physician may wish to see in his office the next day. Finally, the training room must be cleaned and readied for the next day.

It is now hours after fans and players have left the stadium, and professional baseball trainer is finally ready to call it a day. He is ready to go home, perhaps read the professional journals in athletic training to stay abreast of the latest research on injuries and rehabilitation, and then, finally, rest up for the next day to begin. Maybe he'll even have a few minutes with his wife and kids, but there's a high incidence of divorce among athletic trainers.

If this were a road game, the activities and times would be fairly similar, with the exception of the time needed to check and stock the medical trunks for supplies to be taken on the road with the team. A different town or towns, a hotel instead of your own bed, are the basic differences between home and road games for the athletic trainer. He has to love it to be successful.

11

ICING IT DOWN

In the simplest terms, the pitcher's job is to prevent runs from scoring. He does this by executing a plan to counteract the desires of the batter. It is not necessary to throw each pitch by the batter for a strike, though this is certainly a viable strategy. Instead the pitcher can be successful if he keeps the batter from striking the ball solidly, relying on his defense to prevent hits when the ball does enter play. If the pitcher's best friend is the double play, the slow roller has to be a pretty good pal.

Like any job, a pitcher cannot be successful if he does not bring his tools with him to his workplace. He has even less success if he cannot make it to work at all due to injury or fatigue. If pitching to you is more than a hobby—if it is a passion, a need, a must—then keeping your tools at the ready is paramount. These tools are velocity, deception, location, and craft. It is art and science on the mound as any pitcher stands alone, ball in glove, waiting for the sign. But this pitcher is not really alone. He works with his catcher, his defense, his run support, his coaches, and his medical team to keep his tools sharp and ready.

In the summer of 2003 I was sitting in a restaurant with Dr. Rany Jazayerli and two officials from a major league club. During the discussion, Rany brought up something he'd read in the late 1980s about platoon advantages being not just left-right but also groundball-flyball and other various mixes. One official was excited, never having heard this. It was news to me as well, and I left the restaurant wondering what other advantages there might be. When Rany told the story to someone else, the reply was, "They didn't know that?"

There is so much knowledge and wisdom in the game of baseball that some has been lost or at least hidden. Principles popularized by Branch Rickey come back into vogue under Billy Beane, and pitches like the forkball are modified into today's split-finger. Sabermetrics helps us look at baseball in new ways, seeking to improve the game. One easy way to do this is to reassess the old ways and make sure we haven't left something behind.

In researching this book I have discovered an amazing amount of information. Reading through stacks of books, research papers, and discussing pitching with some of the greatest minds and pitchers in the game has been something like studying for a master's degree in Pitchology. Still, from time to time I was left somewhat overwhelmed. Sometimes I was shocked by our lack of knowledge or our lack of answers. So few organizations and coaches are actively seeking better answers and new methods that it will be difficult to bring about change.

Instead of expecting baseball to better itself, as concerned coaches, players, parents, and even fans we must demand better. If the men who are trusted with running the game and with protecting the most precious baseball resources will not change their views, we must show them why change is necessary. By arming ourselves with the best knowledge, we can educate more people and slowly create a revolution in baseball.

Just as pitch counts and sabermetrics have made a slow march into the game over the past few decades, it will not be a quick process. In the battle to save the pitcher, delays will cause many pitchers to fall. We cannot hope to stop pitcher abuse in one fell swoop but must concentrate on winning each small battle. By spreading the word, by educating young players and their coaches, by saving pitchers one at a time, we can minimize the damage.

In an age when more pitchers are injured than in any other period of baseball history, we must support the organizations that do the research and the people who can get the message out. By using the knowledge we have now—much of which I have tried to fit between the covers of this book—we can change the game for the better. Saving the pitcher will save the game we all love.

Acknowledgments

The team at Baseball Prospectus.

Also, Lee Sinins, Tom House, Gary Heil, Tim Marchman, Jim Andrews, Glenn Fleisig, Stan Conte, Jay Jaffe, Alex Belth, Bill James and Matthew Namee, and Aaron Gleeman.

All research for this book and the Gagne game log study were performed by Blake Kirkman, who went above and beyond the call. He's yet another of those underpaid, overworked people who make baseball great. The information on labrum surgery is courtesy of Jay Jaffe and originally appeared on "Futility Infielder" (www.futilityinfielder.com), November 11, 2003.

All injury data, unless otherwise noted, is courtesy of Baseball Prospectus and the Baseball Prospectus Injury Database.

A Pitcher's Education: Suggested Reading

Robert Adair, *The Physics of Baseball* (New York, 2002).
Blending scientific fact and sports trivia, Adair examines what a baseball or player in motion does—and why.

Baseball Graphs (www.baseballgraphs.com).
Website devoted to "baseball at a glance."

Baseball Prospectus (www.baseballprospectus.com).
Articles, statistics, chats, forecasts, and features, updated daily by the BP team.

Alex Belth, *Bronx Banter* (www.all-baseball.com/bronxbanter).
Online columnist, at all-baseball.com.

BP Team of Experts, *Baseball Prospectus 2004* (New York, 2004).
Statistics, analysis, and insight for the information age. Includes performance analysis of more than 1,600 players and includes top 50 prospects, 2003 draft, Minor Leagues, and Rookie Ball.

Harvey Dorfman, *The Mental ABC's of Pitching* (South Bend, Ind., 2000).

A handbook written as an easy-to-use, A-to-Z reference, Dorfman's book addresses the problems every pitcher can face before, during, and after competition and the strategies for solving these problems.

Tom House, *Fit to Pitch* (Champaign, Ill., 1996).
House's pitcher-specific training program details ways to strengthen the body and arm so pitchers can take the mound in top condition.

Tom House, *The Pitching Edge* (Champaign, Ill., 1999).
House offers special instruction and insight into the mechanics, conditioning, and psychology of pitching for superior performance.

Jay Jaffe, Futility Infielder (www.futilityinfielder.com).
Online baseball journal.

Pat Jordan, *A False Spring* (St. Paul, Minn., 1998).
Due to Jordan's inconsistency and lack of control as a minor-league pitcher, the promise of the majors fades away.

Pat Jordan, *The Suitors of Spring* (New York, 1973).
Jordan, a promising young pitcher who never made it to the majors, became a journalist and has here collected his *Sports Illustrated* pieces about pitchers.

Kevin Kerrane, *Dollar Sign on the Muscle* (New York, 1989).
Kerrane explores the world of baseball scouting.

Jane Leavy, *Sandy Koufax: A Lefty's Legacy* (New York, 2003).
The story of the legendary left-handed pitcher.

Michael Lewis, *Moneyball* (New York, 2004).
Here is Lewis's quest for the secret of success in baseball—the business and the game.

Dr. Mike Marshall, *Coaching Pitchers* (available at www.drmikemarshall.com).

Dr. Marshall's online book collects his pitcher training secrets, developed over years of research and coaching.

Leo Mazzone, *Pitch Like a Pro* (New York, 1999).
The pitching coach for the Atlanta Braves offers a guide to young pitchers and their coaches, Little League through high school.

Rob Neyer and Bill James, *The Neyer/James Guide to Pitchers* (New York, 2004).
An historical compendium of pitching, pitchers, and pitches.

Daniel Okrent, *Nine Innings* (Boston, 2000).
Okrent dissects a single baseball game played in June 1982— between the Milwaukee Brewers and the Baltimore Orioles— inning by inning, play by play.

Leroy (Satchel) Paige, *Maybe I'll Pitch Forever* (Lincoln, Nebr., 1993).
The story of the first black pitcher in the American League.

Christian Ruzich, *Cub Reporter* (www.all-baseball.com/cubreporter).
Analyzing the Cubs to death since July 2001, at all-baseball.com.

Pavel Tsatsouline, *Relax into Stretch* (St. Paul, Minn., 2001).
Tsatsouline explains how to regain the buoyant flexibility of a young child while maximizing power and strength.

Pavel Tsatsouline, *Power to the People!* (St. Paul, Minn., 1999).
Using a classified Soviet Special Forces workout, Tsatsouline details how to get super-strong without training to muscle failure or exhaustion.

Pavel Tsatsouline, *The Naked Warrior* (St. Paul, Minn., 2003).
Tsatsouline reveals exactly what it takes to be super-strong in minimum time—when your body is your only tool.

Pavel Tsatsouline, *The Russian Kettlebell Challenge* (St. Paul, Minn., 2001).

Both the Soviet Special Forces and numerous world-champion Soviet Olympic athletes used the ancient Russian kettlebell to turbocharge physical performance. Here is the first-ever complete kettlebell training program.

Craig Wright and Tom House, *The Diamond Appraised* (New York, 1990).

Pitching coach House and statistician Wright team up to approach the game theoretically and practically.

Index

A NOTE ON THE AUTHOR

Will Carroll writes a daily column on player injuries for Baseball Prospectus, the website devoted to baseball analysis. His groundbreaking work in analyzing baseball injuries has brought him national recognition from people inside and outside the game, and has helped general managers and others toward an entirely new perspective on player health. Carroll is also host of Baseball Prospectus Radio. He lives in Indianapolis.